D0302455

Love Hurts

For J. McK. K
ALWAYS

Love Hurts

The True Story of a Life Destroyed

Jeff Randall

MAINSTREAM PUBLISHING

EDINBURGH AND LONDON

Copyright © Jeff Randall, 2008
All rights reserved
The moral right of the author has been asserted

First published in Great Britain in 2008 by
MAINSTREAM PUBLISHING COMPANY
(EDINBURGH) LTD
7 Albany Street
Edinburgh EH1 3UG

ISBN 9781845962982

A catalogue record for this book is available
from the British Library.

Typeset in Biro and Garamond

Printed in Great Britain by
CPI Cox & Wyman, Reading, RG1 8EX

For each man kills the thing he loves,
Yet each man does not die.
– *The Ballad of Reading Gaol*
Oscar Wilde

Acknowledgements

So many to thank and so little space to do so! Where to start?

A huge amount of unquantifiable gratitude goes to the quartet of loyalists who refused to run out when the money did: Mum, Annie, Lea and Dale. I couldn't have done it without you.

To Liam, with more gratitude than there are words in the biggest dictionary – you know why. Keep the green flag flying and proudly follow the Hibs!

To Aaron and Amy just for being part of me. And to Daniel and Kearan for being here, too.

To Kerry. For agreeing that life's too short for hard feelings.

To Uncle John and Auntie Jackie, who've known me longer than I have myself and were there for me in troubled times. I now get the opportunity to express my unequivocal gratitude. Thank you.

To Trevor Kelly and Keith Robertson for your often unappreciated friendship throughout these last 30 years of my life.

To Jenny Brian. Thank you for not judging me when the circumstances of our acquaintance would have made it very easy for you to do so. And for having the confidence in me that I did not have at the time.

To Samantha and Lee for the fags and friendship you gave me during that bleak summer of 2006.

To Karen for making me feel human again and the positive reaction to what is a very brutally honest manuscript. And also for the loan of the elephants. Perhaps it is fitting that they are not here!

And to Gayle. Thank you all for not judging me after reading it. Same to Elaina.

To Stevie J., one of the good guys.

And the guys who have put a smile on my face over the years: Sabs and family, Davie J., Tommy L. (and Carol, too), Willie A. and family, Iain S., the Swanys boys of '91/'92 (I really did appreciate you all but never really said as much), Greig S. and his mum, Mrs S., and of course Les Moore, who was always encouraging and eager to read this book before he sadly died in June 2006.

Thanks also to John McCusker, Mike Cowley and Tom McVittie for their instruction, erudition and enlightenment during my year at Telford – never a dull moment! Thanks are due to my fellow students at Telford (you know who you are), who shared an eventful journey with me.

I am also grateful to have been offered a chance to achieve the previously unachievable by the staff involved with the English and Scottish Literature departments at the University of Edinburgh.

My agent Jenny Brown is one of the finest people I have ever known; I am so lucky to have her representation and her acquaintance.

Thanks to the team at Mainstream, who have taken me through the publishing process with kindness and dignity. Special mentions in this regard are due to Ailsa Bathgate, who probably wishes she had been allocated some other drafts to work with, and the inimitable Fiona Brownlee, a woman who effortlessly combines professionalism with humanity – not an easy task, I'm sure.

Finally, Linda Watson-Brown has been truly magnificent. Not only for being so generous with her professional knowledge, putting hundreds of hours into sorting out my too-big manuscript and offering me the soundest of advice. But most of all for the hugs!

There are no doubt many more who deserve a mention and I do apologise for this temporary bout of amnesia. There are of course also many who will never again be worth more than just a passing thought. I hope you know who you are, too!

Jeff Randall
www.jeffrandall.co.uk
June 2008

Contents

Prologue

All my life, I've felt alone. I've been an outsider looking in, never knowing how to take part but always trying. Until recently, I've never known why I felt this way, where it came from – why was I always the spectator, never the participant? I know some things about myself: I'm a mass of contradictions; I'm permanently uneasy, never content. I'm needy but can't accept anyone who tries to fill that neediness. I'm quiet but loud. Normal on the outside but disturbed underneath. Always looking for the best but always seeing the worst. Now – as I enter a part of my life in which contentment and positive thinking finally seem possible – is the time to reflect on what I am and what has brought me to this point.

This is the story of my life.

The good and the bad.
The love and the hate.
The people and the places.
The give and the take.

Most of all, it's about the truth – the way I see it. It's been a hell of a journey and I'd change much of it if I could, but there are some roads I would always travel, some trips I could not deny myself, no matter what they have done to me.

* * *

11

My story starts in 1990. I was 21. My life was just about to be defined. I had reached my own personal end point. I was finally and completely alone with my own horrors. I pressed the self-destruct button for what I was convinced was to be the last time. I stood high above the ground and jumped, hoping to end it all.

I didn't realise it was just the start.

1

The End

19 AUGUST 1990

I'd like you to come with me, come with me back in time, to witness a certain scene. My journey starts on that early Sunday summer evening in Edinburgh. The weather is nondescript. The streets are quiet; there's very little traffic. The *Chart Show* is playing. A hit from the *Pretty Woman* soundtrack blares out from Radio One. It is somehow appropriate, as wishful thinking is all I had left. But now everything around me is peripheral – all that matters is what I'm about to do. In a few moments, it will all be over.

I've already been out here today, out to stand on this window ledge three blocks up from the ground. The usual arguments have brought me to this place, to this decision. Leanne and I have been at each other's throats again, using the same words, hurting each other in the same ways. But I've found a new way. When I made my first trip out here, she pulled me back from the ledge. She won't do that this time.

The window in the bedroom that faces the street is still open. Still open from the last time I climbed out there. I went out; she brought me back. But now . . .

BANG . . . everything goes white.

I jump.

13

Feet first.

People say that your life flashes before you when you hurtle towards death. It's more complicated than that. I have two people thinking inside my head at the same time. The two sides of my disturbed, fragmented self are both shouting, both trying to make me hear them. I feel as if one part of me is in a glass elevator going down, while another part is in an identical glass lift going up. I go over the past and the present in the few seconds I have left. But I have so little time. The thoughts are racing, banging into each other. One thought is louder than the others.

THIS ISN'T GOING TO WORK.

When I first stepped out onto the window ledge, throwing myself onto the pavement below seemed like a pretty decent means to an end. I knew what the consequences would be but I wouldn't be around to worry about them. Now I know that I've miscalculated. I wasn't high enough to jump. I went feet first. I look down and realise there isn't enough distance between me and the ground. My body is twisted the wrong way – I'm not going the way I need to, my head isn't going to smash into a million pieces before anything else. I panic – even though there isn't time to panic. I try to turn around – even though there isn't time to turn around. I'm in mid-air and I'm hurtling feet first towards the rapidly approaching concrete slabs that I need to kill me. I try to manoeuvre my lower body upwards but I can't. Gravity is now my enemy when it was to be my healer. I'm falling too fast. I feel a brief burning on my face. I've learned that tears fall faster than gravity. The panic is overwhelming. I can't get my head down; I need to be upside down for this to happen, for it to work. No matter how hard I cry and try, I can't move my body at all.

I hit the ground – feet first as I anticipated – then I fall over onto my front. I look around. I'm OK. I'm OK!

I'm not OK.

As I get my head together, I look down. It takes a while to hit me but I finally accept that the white thing I see is my own shin bone coming out of the back of my leg. As soon as I see it, the pain kicks in and I lose all sense of time. I don't notice the people around me yet I know they are there. I hear Leanne say an ambulance is on its way.

The End

I am not dead.

I did not die.

I lie twisted and mutilated on a cold, hard concrete slab. I jumped into oblivion but I failed to reach my planned destination. The irony of it is staggering. I couldn't even manage to die. I've been falling all my life and I wanted to keep falling for ever, and yet my final attempt hasn't worked. A few seconds ago, I wanted to die. Now I know the reality is I just don't want to live. I never have from the moment I started falling, twenty-one and a half years ago.

I'm alive.

Shit.

2

Beginnings

1968

As I fell, I knew that my past had won. It had pushed me to that point. It had controlled my life and was now taking over my future. As I tried to kill myself, I accepted that the fight was over – the irony of later finding myself alive wouldn't be lost on me.

As I fell towards what I was sure was my certain physical death, I knew that the other parts of me had been dead for some time. I couldn't remember a time when I felt whole. Alive. Undead.

Getting rid of the physical me would have just been completing the job.

I wasn't scared of death. It was life that brought terror. And now I'd have to face life again. As I lay on the pavement, I wanted to pass out and I couldn't even look at the tangled mess of my legs. Perhaps I needed to feel the pain; perhaps that's why I was still conscious. I'd always believed that self-harm was a way of showing the world how sore you were. I had pretty obvious scars now.

Leanne kept talking to me until the ambulance arrived, which took almost an hour, as there was a strike on. I heard the driver say that I had multiple injuries but I focused on the one I had seen. The most severe always takes precedence over the others and I could only deal with one thing at a time. I was put on an orange collapsible stretcher and I remember the 'click' as the two parts were slotted into place. As they lifted me, I screamed. Screamed because of the physical pain but also for what I had failed to do, for the mess I had made of something that should have been pretty straightforward. Once in the ambulance, I recognised the route the driver was taking by the roofs and spaces between buildings from the West End up Lothian Road, Earl Grey Street and into Lauriston Place. I watched the streets pass by, upside down and sepia-tinted through the smoked-glass windows as I was given an agonising tour of the city-centre rooftops.

When I got to the Royal Infirmary, I was put in the bed closest to the nurses' station. I was top of the list. I'd managed to get myself to the peak of the fucked-up body hierarchy, which was scant consolation for someone who had wanted life to be over not so long ago.

I was filled with crushing anxiety as the pain hit again and I looked down at my buckled frame. I'd lived with the crap in my head for years and now I'd have to face up to life with a crap body, too. I was hostile, belligerent and uncooperative. I felt that I deserved to be.

I'd felt that way for as long as I could remember.

I came into this world on Hogmanay 1968, although people in the place I was born would barely even recognise the word 'Hogmanay'. I am a Scotsman through and through. To my shame, however, I have an English father and I was born in England.

I didn't know my father: not really, anyway. I wasn't an unexpected consequence of a loveless one-night stand; I was the planned result of a loveless marriage. My mother always wanted children and I was her first. I was a difficult subject for her to practise on. At least she was there, though, unlike my father, who rarely was. I have a few very vague memories of him from my early years. In one, he's drunk and swaying from a top-flat sash window with my equally drunk grandfather and uncle at his back. I was with my mum and maternal granny, who were mortified at this performance and who gave the men a humiliating tongue-lashing from the street below. My granny was formidable. She was also the loveliest, most loving and fair-minded woman I have ever known. She was the boss but, most importantly for me, she was also my friend. I didn't have her in my life nearly long enough. Things would have turned out very differently if her life had not been cut short when I was seven years old. But I'm getting ahead of myself.

My father was a seaman, a telecommunications operator with the Royal Navy, which is why I was born near Portsmouth. He was away from home a lot by the time home had become Edinburgh. I don't remember much about our residence in East Hermitage Place but I do remember the next address in Bonnington Road, because that was the place where the drunken menfolk were put in their place by my granny. Bearing in mind that these moves took place before I was two, it is hardly surprising that I have very few recollections. One thing that is certain though is the fact that my father was hardly ever there. We moved again (this time to Balfour Street) while I was still two and this is where my first real memories begin.

The last childhood memory I have of my father is also my first bad memory. As a child, I slept in a tiny unlit boxroom just off my parents' bedroom. On one particular Sunday morning (I know it was a Sunday as there was always a Boys' Brigade march in our street on that day), the door, normally left ajar to allow sunlight in, was slammed shut, leaving me in darkness. I began crying for it to be reopened just enough to let the light back in and, after a while, my mum obliged and I settled down again. Before much longer, however, my father approached my door and slammed it shut again in anger. This time, I screamed, terrified of the unknown and also because I had picked up on the atmosphere coming from my parents' room. Again, my mum opened the door and peace was restored. Not for long. This charade was repeated a few more times but, inevitably, something had to give.

Eventually, I climbed out of my cot, opened the door and stood silently, defiantly, at the foot of my parents' bed. Unwittingly, I'd fought back against unfair authority, a trait that would often prove to be my downfall. My father was a small man. Small men with any sort of power are not a good combination and I could sense something of the sort even at two years old. As far as I remember, this situation fizzled out on that particular morning and, even at that age, I felt I'd beaten him. It was the first confrontation I'd had with either of my parents. It wouldn't be the last.

I staggered through the next few years unspectacularly and my little sister, Lucy, joined the cast. My mum and dad didn't stick together, though. I never did find out the cause of their break-up and even now, having heard both sides of what is really a non-story, I'm none the wiser other than knowing that there was another woman on the scene – another woman who had two kids already. Maybe they were better kids than us. Maybe he liked them more than his own.

I was raised by my mother and spent my younger years listening to her forthright opinions: opinions steeped in bitterness about my dad, which only alienated me further. After he left for good, when four became three, I felt that I was the one that made a crowd. There was no ostensible reason for it but I felt alone. It felt as if I had been discarded. I had to fight for my mum's attention when Lucy arrived and attempt to make sense of my father's absence once he disappeared. As far as I was concerned, I was to blame. Maybe I was. Perhaps becoming a father was a step too far for my father to take. He was young and maybe fatherhood wasn't on his agenda. His desertion was hard to accept whatever the reason; in fact, I'd carry the pain of his rejection for many decades to come and the damage it would cause would be enormous.

With my father gone, my mother embarked upon a self-styled life of parental martyrdom, claiming throughout my childhood that she had sacrificed her life in order to raise my sister and me.

SACRIFICE.

We would have that word branded into our minds as we grew.

It'd be fair to say my mother, like many others, was not a natural. Sadly, she believed she was. As I've grown older and experienced many dark things, I've become convinced that my mother suffered some sort of illness or imbalance. Certainly it's not something I could put a label on but I do know how her behaviour affected me as a child and how it continued to affect the adult I was to become. She was often irrational and sometimes violent.

19

I started school in the summer of 1973 and until then I'd never really encountered the extent of my mum's dark side. The violent, furious ball of rage that would become all too evident in the years ahead hadn't yet been fully witnessed. I know that until I left nursery and started at Holy Cross Roman Catholic Primary, life was fairly uneventful. If anything, my mother was the epitome of a loving single mum of two. Perhaps a bit skint, struggling to make ends meet, but hardly out of the ordinary. I recall her having a job in Boots on Princes Street when I was at nursery. That job was one of only two proper jobs my mum has had in my entire lifetime, neither of which lasted more than a few months – something which somehow was always twisted into being the fault of Lucy and me. The truth, in my eyes, is that she always used being a mum as an excuse not to work. It seemed easier for us to become experts in the benefit system instead. She could have done so much better. Whilst seeming perfectly normal to the outside world, my mum had little sense of real responsibility. Soon we were in the poverty trap: hiding behind what little furniture we had when the bailiffs were peering through the net curtains at the window. I remember thinking it was funny, like a game, even though my mother was drained of all colour. To this day, she says that my father never made any financial contribution to our upkeep. She claims that her refusal of visitation rights was because she felt unable to trust him with either of us, had he expressed an interest. If my father had the same attitude to children that I had in my 20s, then I would have to say that was a fairly wise call. How this affected us materially was the price we as a family had to pay. No access – for whatever reason – equalled no money.

Neither of my parents has been able to explain properly what exactly happened in the early 1970s. One thing I am fairly sure of is the fact that my mother never loved her husband. I think she wanted someone to have kids with and then sit back, do the mum thing, safe in the knowledge that a steady wage would be rolling in at the end of the month. Love didn't come into it, from what I can tell. Throughout my life, until very recently, my mother would regularly tell me, usually in a fit of anger, how big a bastard my father was: he was a snake, a low-life piece of scum who belonged in a sewer – all this was repeated ad nauseam. She'd inevitably follow her rant with one of her favourite lines: 'You, you're your father's son all over.'

While she may have been right about him, she should have let me discover the truth for myself. Yes, my dad is, frankly, a right bastard. But all my mother ever did was create a mystique about him. He was a subject never to be broached except on her terms – usually in rage while I was receiving 'discipline'. I grew up needing my dad. Knowing something huge was missing from within me, I wanted, needed, my dad to love me. I felt rejected and I didn't know why. I started to fall just a wee bit quicker. Although I now have many of the answers, it has taken a lifetime of being hurt by love, or the lack of it, to find them.

Whatever the truth of the matter, and only my parents really know, the fact is that we were permanently skint, living well below the so-called breadline. I hated it. Always hungry, often dirty and perpetually unkempt, wearing other people's cast-offs. My hatred of the second-hand clothes industry remains to this day and when my own kids came along, I certainly overcompensated materially. I never wanted them going through what I did. Money, and the acquisition of money at all costs, became a fixation with me at that young age. It still is – it always will be. Poverty is hell – I should know. It is often said that money can't buy happiness and to a certain extent I'd agree. However, having nothing is a sure-fire way to misery. Having been in both situations, I would take the unskint option every time. Money gives opportunities. Poverty brings frustration and impotence, which brings me back to my mum again.

The first time I recall incurring the full extent of her rage was not long after I started school: I'd only have been about four years old. I'd been sent to the local corner shop for a newspaper and, when there, I had used 2p of the change to buy her a Mars Bar, as I knew that she loved them. I only wanted to make my mum happy. When I gave it to her, she put her face into mine, screaming obscenities, grabbing me and shaking me. She went crazy, a woman possessed. A wee boy who mistakenly spent tuppence! That day marked a significant point in my life. It was the start of the psychological warfare my mum and I would engage in for years to come. The battleground was drawn. The really nasty stuff was just around the corner and would accelerate the descent even more. Before that, however, I wanted out. I tried to spend as little time as possible in the house. I was to become, as my mother had started to describe me, a defiant little bastard. I might have been young but already I knew how to wind her up.

Living on the ground floor of a tenement made it easy for me to escape. I'd regularly be out of the window and round the park in no time at all. One day I saw a group of boys playing football and was desperate to join in. When I was told to be the official 'spectator', I was chuffed. I had a title, a purpose. I was part of the team – they must have really liked me. It didn't take long for the penny to drop. I was alone. I was alone in a crowd. A target at home; a nobody elsewhere. Why did I not seem to matter? After 'spectating' for long enough, my insides trembling, I jumped off the park bench I had been warming, straight into a pile of runny dog shit. I didn't even notice, as I just wanted to go away, away somewhere, anywhere. Anywhere but the park and anywhere but home. Suddenly I was noticed and the taunts began: 'Smelly.' 'Shitey leg.' 'Scabby arse.' 'Look at the manky wee bastard trying to get away.' The crowd of boys were screaming and laughing at me and my shit-encrusted leg. I turned to run and slammed straight into my mum, who had dragged Lucy out to look for me. Cue the inevitable verbal bollocking and subsequent 'doing'. I wanted love and I wasn't getting it. I wanted out.

3

When Love Dies

17 OCTOBER 1976

I'm alone again – this time in a room full of relatives, in a room reeking of antiseptic disinfectant, surrounded by people who ignore me. I'm in a hospital and I've just had my first experience of death, of loss, of having my innards ripped out of my body.

The body on the bed was the centre of my universe.

My granny – gone.

Gone for good.

I might have thought I was alone before, but I am now.

Because of Annie Jeffrey, I know I can be loved, for she adored me. I was her favourite: I know that. All my family know that. In an instant, now that she has died, I lose my faith in love – and yet I need it, need to be loved, to feel loved. I'm desperate for it. To be loved instinctively, the way my granny loved me. I need to love and be loved but I feel abandoned and rejected. My dad is long gone and now my granny has followed him. Different reasons, same result.

In this sterile room full of strangers, I can't work out what place I hold. They all have their own misery to deal with; they're visibly distraught. I am silent. I fix my eyes on my granny's body for a final time. My stomach retches but I'm not sick. I turn to leave the room.

23

This is my pain, my loss, not theirs. They don't count. She was my best friend – mine. Not theirs.

The others follow me out of the room. This seems appropriate to me, as I was Annie's number one. I always came first with her. I shuffle slowly towards the nearest exit. I'm barely aware of the sobs of others. I see a signpost directing people down a dimly lit corridor. It screams out at me. It is not a word I should be familiar with, yet somehow I know the meaning of it.

The signpost is here for me.

It says 'ISOLATION'.

4

Isolation

1976

I wasn't allowed to attend my granny's funeral, as it was considered to be too upsetting an event for me to cope with. Nobody asked me. I wanted to be there. I needed to be there but who was going to listen to a seven-year-old boy?

I was devastated when she died. She was the only person who made my life bearable; she rescued me from the insanity I called home. When I was with her, I felt like the most important person in the world; she lit my life up with a love so easy that I lived for the time I could spend with her. She must have known about the problems at home but it never affected our relationship. To this day, I've never been able to find that same level of happiness, of painless love, with another person. I'm still looking. Perhaps it only ever happens once. Perhaps I want it too much. My grandmother was my first guardian angel and she made my dark world a much brighter place.

When I was with my granny, I could relax and be the little boy I was. I could play, I could run, I could jump, I could laugh, I could say anything that came into my head and be whoever I wanted to be. Often we would walk to Waverley Station and get on whatever train happened to be leaving. We would end up in places all over the country, not worrying about anything at all. If we missed the return service, my granny would just book us into a local guesthouse for the night. I loved those trips and was an enthusiastic train traveller. I'd sit in the carriage with my face stuck to the windows. I was fascinated by the rhythm of the engine wheels beating on the rails beneath. Even now that sound evokes in me the memory of true happiness.

As a small boy, weekends, and Saturdays in particular, were my favourite days of the week. This was when I shared the happiest of times with my granny. In her house, we would be together, just us, because Saturday was Grandad's day for the pub and the bookies. We'd do simple things. She lived in a one-bedroom flat: the same house my mum and her brothers had been raised in. It had the most basic of facilities but none of that mattered. In the main room, which served as a living-room/kitchen, with a bed in the recess, there was a double sink at the window. The wee sink was for everyday use and the larger one, which remained for most of the time covered with a wooden lid, was deep enough to double up as a bath for little people. I remember being bathed by my granny and then wrapped up in a huge towel before she would sit me on her knee, both of us drinking tea from real mugs, and settle down in front of the black and white telly to watch *World of Sport* or *Grandstand.* Granny was a real sports fan: a Celtic supporter who enjoyed showjumping, wrestling, tennis and rugby. It was on one of those dreich Saturdays that I recall being all cosy beside my granny as she explained the intricacies of a Scotland v. Wales rugby international on the telly. I remain the only member of my family to maintain a keen interest in most sports, a fine legacy from that woman who loved me so much.

When a child has been neglected and unloved, when he has dealt with physical and verbal violence from such a young age, the kind of interaction I had with my granny matters. I'm inclined to agree with the celebrated maxim that asserts 'Give me the child until he is seven and I will show you the man.' It lays the ground for the man he will become. While society ignores these children, turns a blind eye and prefers to not notice, the child grows and learns that he is worthless, that he is undeserving of love. Raised like this, that child also learns that he is on his own. These are lessons that create the adults we become. Annie Jeffrey taught me another lesson. That I was worthy of love. That I mattered for who I was. That there was a different kind of life out there if I could only find it. Her death and the loss of that message simply reinforced to me that I was insignificant. I learned the wrong lesson, and I learned it well.

On the day my granny died, I lost my faith in love, yet love on any level would be what I'd crave for the rest of my life. In the years that have passed since then, I've been unable to keep the things I loved the most, and considered most important, close to me. I grew to mistrust those who said they loved me for fear of losing that love. I couldn't allow myself to be loved completely, as completely as my grandmother had loved me, as losing that kind of love was catastrophic and I couldn't have dealt with a loss like that ever again. I would push the love away before it could be taken from me. That self-destructive impulse grew within me from that day onwards.

On 17 October 1976, aged seven years and ten months, I locked the love behind a solid steel door and threw the key away.

On the day my granny's body was taken to her final resting place, it had been arranged that my sister Lucy and I would be looked after by an elderly couple who were friends of the family. I really resented this, as I felt that I should have been allowed to attend the funeral. I deserved to go. I was seven: I was vulnerable, alone and hurting badly, with nowhere to put the pain. Regardless of my age, I needed some form of closure.

Harry was a tall man with a military gait and a deep, commanding voice. I did know him a bit but wasn't particularly close to him. He was a heavy smoker and had a large collection of ornamental lighters displayed in a cabinet in the living room of his flat. I was fascinated by the lighters and picked one up and attempted to light it. Alerted by the scratching of the flint, without warning this giant of a man went ballistic. In one smooth movement, he snatched the lighter from me with his left hand as his right simultaneously leathered me several times across my face, using both the palm and back of his hand in a swishing fashion. He never said a word and the hitting finally stopped when his wife intervened, imploring him to 'leave the laddie alone'. Harry

27

straightened up as if nothing had happened and carefully placed his precious lighter back in the cabinet. I'm still not really sure just what exactly I did to instigate such a brutal reaction but at the time I know I thought that I must have deserved it. I just accepted it must have been my fault again. The blows had stung and my cheeks were throbbing but I didn't cry. I was stunned – bemused yet again by the propensity of adults for violence – but also defiant. Holding my tears in check was a deliberate refusal to give the miserable old bastard the satisfaction of seeing me break down. Anyway, in my experience, crying only ever seemed to send the grown-ups off again and make things worse. No doubt the big guy was proud of himself for imposing some discipline on a confused wee boy whose entire universe had collapsed five days previously.

That night, I told my mum what had happened to me at the hands of Harry. I wanted her to hold me, to say she'd deal with him, to tell me she loved me and would always fight for me. It didn't happen. She was completely uninterested and did nothing about it. I was alone, abandoned, and I'd never been able to rely on her in the past, anyway. The patterns of my life were making themselves clear by now and I was learning that disappointment was all I could rely on.

5

Mummy Dear

1977

In the early part of 1977, my mother bought a flat in the St Leonard's area of Edinburgh. It was on the ground floor of a Victorian tenement, with its own main door. There was also a back door, which led into the stair where my grandad now lived alone in his own flat on the first floor. I had spent a great deal of time in my grandparents' house while Granny was alive and my fondest memories at this time revolved around this place, so, to begin with, I was very pleased to be moving there. My mum said she wanted to return to the place of her birth to take care of her now widowed father – laudable sentiments indeed, if the situation hadn't been so ridiculous. My mum was struggling to look after herself and her children, hindered further by the lack of assistance from my dad. Attempting to take care of an old man as well was as ambitious as it was impossible. If truth be told, the real reason for the move was to enable my mum to be near her dad in her own hour of need, but with this cover story, for once, she had nothing to be ashamed of.

Within weeks of the move, living in squalor with no money, very little food, no heating and sleeping rough on what floorboards hadn't been ripped up, the pressure really began to tell on the three of us.

29

Following the death of my granny, my mum had descended into her own madness. The self-imposed circumstances she now found herself in pushed the cracks in her own sanity further and further apart. It was only a matter of time before the monster in her would be unleashed.

My mother's slide wasn't helped by the lack of input from my dad. He'd been away from us for years and I'd developed a deeply rooted need for him. He'd played no active part in my emotional formation (other than the negative influence of his absence) and this lack of a dad exacerbated my lack of self-worth. Because my mum only ever referred to him in a derogatory way ('bastard by birth, bastard by nature'), usually in a rage of temper directed at me, I'd been blaming myself for years.

At school, I would make up stories to explain his absence. Some of the taller tales involved me saying he had 'died in the Second World War'. Thankfully, none of my peers at school were savvy when it came to historical details – or arithmetic. While, initially, I didn't envy the other kids in my class at school, I was genuinely very curious as to what exactly a 'dad' was. Most of them always referred to having a 'mum*and*dad' (it always seemed to be one word). These kids also seemed to be cleaner than me, better dressed and much more confident. They behaved naturally while I developed various personas as I began to adapt to the circumstances of my life. To them, having a 'mum*and*dad' was the most natural thing in the world; to me, it was an exotic luxury. Somehow I knew I was different but not in a way I could express. My dad had fucked off and got away scot-free. My mum, in all fairness, had been left holding the babies and for that, for staying and coping as best she could, she'll always be afforded immense credit.

I suppose I became the physical outlet for her frustrations. While on the outside she appeared to be a loving, caring, protective parent, behind closed doors things of insignificance could quickly become a full-blown crisis. She could be a vicious tyrant, not only with her hands and feet but also with her tongue. I had to be careful not to upset her in the house, as the slightest thing could carry a severe price. At seven years old, I was fast becoming an expert in domestic diplomacy.

I learned not to criticise anything, particularly our living conditions, but by now I truly despised the new house, as it looked like the inside of a junk-shop storeroom. The rooms were all in various states of disrepair and the whole house was filthy, with a stench of raw decay. The kitchen in particular was caked in grime. We had no washing machine, so what clothes we had were given the odd cursory hand wash in cold water. There was no fridge, no television and not even casings on the electrical fittings. There were crappy things lying about everywhere, which we were told were 'antiques'. There were no carpets or curtains and the previous owner's dodgy patterned wallpaper was peeling off from the walls.

For a few years, all three of us slept in the large back bedroom, initially in the same bed until I eventually preferred a sleeping bag on the floor. The house was always freezing, even in the summer, and at night I would hear my mum telling my sister to breathe deeply under the covers in order to generate some heat. Dirty dishes would lie unwashed for days in a heap in the kitchen sink, submerged in scum-covered cold water only to eventually be given a complacent wipe with a manky old towel at mealtimes. These mealtimes were always erratic. Teacups were permanently tanned on the inside and the ancient metal cutlery showed advanced signs of corrosion. We were, in effect, squatting in our own house. I knew this wasn't a normal way to exist. Lucy and I were dressed in second-hand clothes or other people's cast-offs. These rags sometimes had a once-weekly dip in the kitchen sink on the same day (usually a Sunday) that all three of us shared the bathwater.

I was sent to school dressed in short trousers long after everyone else. The reason given for this decision was that I was likely to rip long trousers at the knees, so it would be shorts whether I liked it or not. I was also made to wear big, clumpy, unfashionable shoes, often with the soles flapping – many an evening would be spent heating a knife blade in the one bar of my grandad's gas fire as attempts were made to reunite the rubber with the leather. Inevitably, I was the subject of much ridicule at school, although I quickly found a way to combat the taunts and catcalls.

Surprisingly, my weapon of choice wasn't violence but humour. I became sharp-tongued, with a calculated self-deprecating streak, managing somehow to turn the slagging on its head.

Back at home, my mum filled the house with all sorts of junk, some of it bought from jumble sales, some from second-hand shops and some even lifted from the bins on the night before collection day. A succession of dodgy workmen traipsed through the house, invariably disappearing before completing the jobs they had been asked to do. There were live electrical wires exposed at all the light fittings and power points, which meant that I took my life into my hands every time I tried to read something for school. I would tentatively put the light on and on many an occasion was rewarded with a 240-volt arm-numbing shock for my troubles. There were loose and missing floorboards throughout the house that would be the cause of many minor injuries. Not only was the place at this time a ramshackle old hovel, it was also a death trap.

My mum had an odd idea of taste and she would deny the squalor by describing various areas of the house with phrases like 'breakfast bar', 'shower room' and 'en-suite'. If you had seen my mother in the street, you would never have guessed the conditions she lived in. She always looked clean and presentable, even if her kids were a pair of scruffy ragamuffins. To use her own words, words she would use to describe me in later life as I became all things to all people, she was a 'show parade'. No surprises where I got that from, I always thought when she threw that jibe at me.

Mealtimes were an adventure into the unknown, as my mother's attempts at cooking were lamentable; indeed, she freely admits now that she chose to be a lousy cook. It was a case of whatever happened to be to hand in the cupboard being thrown into a large blackened pot and heated on the hob until it bubbled. Us kids would be clueless as to the contents of the mixture but there always seemed to be beans of some description in there – beans and 'black bits'. Black bits that my mum would attempt to pass off as raisins, currants or other such nonsense.

One Sunday, when faced with a greasy plate filled with a rancid brown sludge that tasted worse than it looked (quite an achievement), I point-blank refused to eat it. Knowing that there would be a penalty to pay and in order that I could get the whole performance over with as quickly as possible, I asked my mum, with tears welling up in my eyes: 'May I please leave the table, Mummy dear?' (She was always obsessed with observing the niceties of Victorian-style etiquette.) By this time, I had suffered a few healthy doings at her hands but nothing could have prepared me for what happened next. At first, I was refused permission to leave the table and coldly told that if I didn't eat it I would be 'baptised' in it. All I could do was shake my head as the tears came thick and fast. She moved towards me, blocking off any escape route, and repeated herself. I didn't react. 'Last chance,' she now angrily stated. 'Are you going to eat your dinner?' I was trembling with a raw fear but I just said as apologetically as I could that I was unable to eat it, as it was disgusting. 'Sorry,' I repeated over and over, again and again.

I could see the red mist had descended as I looked into my mum's eyes and all I could do was wait for the explosion. After what could have been hours but was more likely seconds, nothing happened. The violence didn't come. Confident enough to believe the moment had passed when she removed my plate from the table, moving it in such a way as to suggest she was taking it to the washing-up basin, I momentarily relaxed. As I exhaled with relief, her free hand grabbed my long hair and in one deft, expertly executed movement she proceeded to hammer my face into the plate, so the blood now pouring from my nose was lost in the food staining my face. I tried to get away but her grasp of my hair was far too strong.

Maintaining her vice-like grip on my hair, she dragged me to my feet, all the while screaming hostilities in my face. I lost my balance and dragged her down with me as I fell to the floor. She was quicker to her feet than I was and she started to lay into me as I tried to scramble away on all fours. My destination was the back door and out into the common stair, as I knew, no matter what, my mum would never perform in public.

As I reached the narrow hallway, I slipped again and, with blood and snot mixed in with the shit I had refused to eat dripping from my face, for a crucial moment I was blinded. The hand was back, fiercer now, regaining a firm grip on my hair in order to launch another assault. Her free hand struck me in the stomach, kidneys, neck and back before she started swinging my head from wall to wall by the hair. She was screaming at me as I was screaming at her to stop. The noise was unbearable but it only served to refuel my mother's anger and give her a second wind.

I had to stop her bouncing me off the walls, so I put my hands up over my head to protect my now patchy, bleeding scalp. As I fell, I felt a kick and a stamp as I lay helpless at the back door. I don't remember her stopping; I must have passed out with pain or fear.

It remains little wonder that my mum hadn't the energy to work when she required everything to be held in reserve to knock the living fuck out of me.

6

Exchanges

1977

On Saturday, when most kids were playing or going to football with their dads, my sister and I would be dragged along to a jumble sale or two. I hated them as much as my mum seemed to love them. She thrived on the atmosphere in those smelly church halls bursting with old women fighting over trash disguised as 'bargains'.

Whatever pile of crap was purchased would then in the week ahead be hawked around various local dealers. Surely, I often used to think, it would be easier to go out and find a proper job.

Some of the dross my mum bought at the weekends was taken to a building in George Street known as 'the school exchange'. Basically, it was a place where second-hand clothing could be traded for school uniforms, shoes and other things. Lucy and I were real-life second-hand roses and it felt horrible.

On one visit to the school exchange, a door that led out into a small back street had been left ajar and the sound of children playing could be heard clearly. Never one to miss an opportunity, my mum gleefully explained in great detail to my sister and I that not only did this dreadful place deal in clothes and shoes but under certain circumstances they would trade in children as well. She went on to tell us that we were both on the list to be swapped for a 'good boy or girl' if at any time we were bad. If we didn't toe the line, we would be taken from her and put in a cage where we would have to learn to behave in the hope that we would perhaps be taken in by a childless family. This talent for telling stories would be one of her many legacies to me.

Stories, however, come in many shapes and forms and one of the few positive results of the jumble-sale jaunts was that I was never short of reading material. I'd been a keen reader for as long as I could remember and it wasn't long into my school career that their books stopped being enough to nourish me. The jumble sales reaped no end of comics – *Victor, Dan Dare, Beano, Dandy, Topper, Look and Learn, Hotspur, Victor, Valiant* and my favoured football publications, *Shoot, Scorcher and Score, Tiger* and, of course, the all-time greatest, *Roy of the Rovers.*

However, the best source of decent books was Grandad's bedside press. 'Faither' (as he became affectionately known to me) was an extremely intelligent and well-read man, although mainly self-taught. His formal education, such as it was, had ended by the time he was twelve years old – a time in his life when he had already been working for three years. He delighted in some fairly meaty literature and could effortlessly recite all manner of poetry. In the mid-1970s, he took me along to the Assembly Rooms in George Street, where Hugh MacDiarmid was giving a recitation. I remember being captivated by this strange man, who looked like he brushed his hair with a toffee apple, as he laid forth his words in a strident, rambunctious fashion. An ephemeral electricity crackled as a reverential hush descended on the vast hall, and when I looked at Grandad's face as we stood at the back behind the sea of chairs (I'm sure he knew someone who got us in for nothing – Grandad knew lots of people), I realised he was even more mesmerised than I was.

On the only occasion I remember being ill (as opposed to injured) as a child, I was in Grandad's bed with measles, glumly bored out of my spotty face. With trepidation, I got out of bed and approached a stack of books. In amongst the Gazetteers of Scotland, Walter Scotts, Robert Burnses and Rudyard Kiplings was a small, innocuous, beige hardbound book with no dust jacket. Curious, I picked it up and on opening it was fascinated by an illustration of a small boy holding out a bowl to a ferocious-looking fat man. *Oliver Twist* was the first proper book I ever read and from that moment onwards, as I scurried back to the big bed, my love affair with the written word was elevated to a higher level.

I am pleased to say this is one relationship that has afforded me no disappointment whatsoever.

7

Falling

1977–79

In 1977, when I was eight, I suffered severe facial injuries in an accident – a genuine one for a change. I was being hurried out of the house by my mum so that we would make the start of yet another bloody jumble sale. Without having to think twice, I was off, straight across the road. I ran into Holyrood Park, where two local lads I knew were messing around. We climbed the grassy slope leading up to the Salisbury Crags. The two older boys got to the top of some rocks in seconds but I got myself stuck halfway up. I passed out with fear and fell. I landed, unconscious, on the large boulders below, the brunt of the impact being borne by the left-hand side of my face.

I have no memory of being taken to and examined in the Sick Kids Hospital. The left side of my face had been ripped apart by the fall (or the landing), leaving the right side amazingly untouched. I had, unbelievably, sustained no other injuries at all. When I was brought into A&E, waiting with another patient was a Dutch plastic surgeon who was visiting Edinburgh on holiday. When she saw the extent of the damage to my face, she approached my mother and introduced herself. I have no clue as to how hospital protocol works but this surgical genius was allowed to operate on me. The woman was magnificently talented and although directly after the operation my face resembled the *Batman* villain Two-Face, with 104 dark-blue cat-gut stitches holding the flaps of flesh together, within a few months it would be virtually impossible to spot any damage at all.

After the operation, I began to enjoy the attention I received. I was even written about in the local newspaper. I quickly realised that visible signs of pain were almost guaranteed to win sympathy. It was something I would remember for the rest of my life: *this* was how you got attention.

The nature of the damage done was strangely appropriate. I had two faces in one, depending on which profile was prominent. The monster within had begun to manifest but I was the only one aware of it. To the outside world, I was relatively normal – I had learned the art of duplicity and denial quickly and effectively.

When I was sent home to recover further, it was one of the few periods in my early life when my mum actually did real 'mum' things. She fussed around me, excelling herself in her care of me. Nothing was too much trouble and I took full advantage of the situation by having her run around, constantly catering for my every whim. It was great. I had juice, sweets, crisps and comics whenever I wanted. In the past, when I had been absent from school for reasons of ill health, my mum had handed the duty of care over to her own parents. This time, however, the boat was pushed out further than ever before. I couldn't believe that my mum was looking after me properly. For once, I felt really close to her, as she did a grand job. In the two months or so that it took for me to heal, she managed to keep her own demons at bay. I just wish that they had gone for ever.

By the time I returned to school after my extended summer holiday, things had reverted pretty much back to abnormal. The physical beatings and mind games increased: even the cat would get a leathering if he had the audacity to bring in his latest catch from outside. There seemed to be some sort of synchronicity involved. On the days building up to every fourth Sunday, things were at their most stressful. The house was deteriorating by the month, although I was now fairly immune to the dire conditions in which I lived. I spent as much time as possible playing in the streets with the local kids.

For most kids, schooldays were a bit of a drag. For me, it was the opposite. School was a safe place. Although my early school years had seen name-calling and ostracism, in time I'd grown into a reasonably popular child. I was a half-decent mimic, probably because I preferred to hide behind the persona of somebody else, and I was always ready with a quick put-down. I'd rather be the first to take the piss out of myself and pre-empt any cruel strike from others.

Now my mum withdrew me from Holy Cross Primary after an incident in which I stole a bottle of milk from the crate of leftover free milk distributed to the class. The incident was blown way out of all proportion and in any event the school was miles away from where we now lived. It was decided that I would spend my final year in primary education at a local non-denominational school.

In spite of my appearance, I employed the same techniques as I had at my previous school and fitted in reasonably quickly. Inexplicably, I even made the starting 11 in the football team. Lessons with my new teacher, Mr Thompson, were much more fun than anything I had ever known in a classroom. He was a gifted teacher with a superb ability to educate and entertain, and I responded well to this new approach.

The bad boy in me would occasionally surface. One Monday, whilst walking to school with a mate who was in the year below me, we decided to bunk off, neither of us having ever done so before. My mate, Ian, had procured a tenner from home (quite a haul in 1979) and so, between us, we decided it would be good fun to have a nice day out even though the weather was awful. We jumped on a bus and headed out of town to Dalkeith. After wandering around aimlessly for a wee while in the pissing rain, spending Ian's loot on a football and a huge bag of sweeties, we headed for Dalkeith Adventure Park. We quickly lost track of time as we sickened ourselves on the sweets and when I realised how late it must be getting, I began to panic about my mum finding out. She always collected Lucy from school and would expect me to be at least somewhere in the area. I couldn't very well go back to the school and walk out the gates as if I had been there all day but neither could I go straight home. I was fucked. Eventually, I chose the only real option available to me and went to my grandad's house, because I reckoned he would stop my mum going over the score if she kicked off. Ian came along with me, as he too was in fear of returning home.

My mum was already at my grandad's house when I knocked on the door. My grandad answered and let both of us into the small flat. Once inside, the air instantly turned several shades of blue. Had I any idea of the fuckin' worry I had caused my mother? I was a fuckin' stupid, selfish boy and anything could have happened to me; where the fuck had I been anyway? And on and on and on. It was my grandad doing the shouting this time. I had heard the stories about his temper but, while I could see that he was a formidably strong man, I'd never seen him wound up like this. He was shaking with anger, working his fury up into the most heated of frenzies. And then, when the temperature gauge reached the top: BANG! He slapped me, open-handed with one of his celebrated huge meaty shovels, right across the face at full strength. He only struck me the once but it was more than enough. Ian was rooted to the spot, bracing himself, with real fear in his rapidly filling eyes. He was anticipating a blow that never came. My grandad knew his place and would never have struck another person's child but Ian had no way of knowing that.

In the end, I was glad that my grandad hadn't punched me: the slap was sore but not quite as hard as a fist, which could have knocked my head off. I was learning more and more, faster and faster. Violence was acceptable. Violence was powerful. Violence worked.

8

Little Victories

1979–80

Around this time, my mother had managed to get what was to be her last real job. All the childcare duties were passed to my grandad until at least six o'clock on weekday evenings. One afternoon, he asked me if I fancied going out anywhere. I told him that I'd really like to go for a proper haircut in the barber's shop. I'd always had to rely on my mum doing it with blunt scissors or hand-powered rusty clippers. My hair was always lank and greasy, and I really wanted to see what I would look like if it was cut properly.

My grandad agreed and took me to the barber's halfway up St Mary's Street, just around the corner from the Royal Mile. I sat patiently in the shop, waiting amongst the silent throng of men. This was a completely new experience for me. Normally, I associated shops and the like with the world of women. This was different: it was a lot quieter for a start, as the waiting patrons sat reading a variety of newspapers and pornography, sucking deeply on their Regal King Size. Words exclusive to the male world were everywhere: words like 'Brylcreem', 'Durex' and 'Mayfair'. Even the smells in the shop were new to me. I loved it. I wanted so much to leave my childhood behind and be a permanent part of that man's world. Things would be different when *I* was a man, I told myself.

'Crew cut, please,' I said to the bald barber before my grandad could say anything. I sat on the wooden platform the barber had affixed to his big red leather chair and watched as he expertly shaved my hair almost to the 'wood'. It made me look like a regular boy for the first time in my life. As my grandad paid the man for his efforts, I did hear him mutter under his breath, 'Christ knows what your bloody mother's going to say when she sees you.' Not only had I made the decision to get my hair cut but I had also been given the right to choose the one style I knew my mum would dislike the most, as she'd no longer be able to grab me by my hair.

On her arrival at my grandad's, her reaction was predictably one of anger but I detected the impotence as she ranted in vain at both my grandad and me. Neither of us was bothered. We both knew that no matter how much she shouted, it wouldn't bring my hair back. Like any decent fighter, though, my mum would come back stronger, more astute, with new tactics to deploy and new techniques to experiment with.

Predictably enough, my mum left her job not long after the haircut incident, blaming me. She claimed that I was causing my grandad no end of trouble, so she would make the sacrifice again and devote all her time to looking after me. It would have been laughable if it weren't so pathetic. I have tried to remember any significant conflict between my grandad and me around this time and come up blank. If anything, things were much more normal. We were clean, cooked for and stimulated properly in his house, and as a bonus my mum was too tired to dish out any spontaneous violence. Although still being dragged to jumble sales on Saturdays and church on Sundays, life was as hassle-free as it was ever going to be. With my mum no longer working, things were about to revert back to the normality of unpredictability and disorder.

Perhaps my memory is playing tricks on me but the only reason I could see for my mum quitting was that a job was too normal for her. The chaos of her house of horrors had become her comfort zone, even if it was a comfort zone full of squalor and junk. Maybe she derived some meaning from it.

By now, with me having reclaimed some control of my own life with my baldy head, my mum resorted mainly to verbal attacks. I would match her word for word, as I was losing my fear the older I got. My hair was no longer working to cover my face and it was completely exposed as the mirror image of my dad – the bastard son of my father, as my mum enjoyed labelling me.

She would say I was scum, scum that had been sent from Hell to punish her for all her sins. I was a defiant little bastard, a selfish shitehouse who didn't appreciate just how much she had sacrificed for me. I could go on and on with variations on the theme but the real problem was that I looked like my father. I was a constant reminder to her of her failure not only as a mother but perhaps as a wife as well.

She was often torn – for example, it was in the spirit of wanting the best for me that she submitted my name to be considered to sit the entrance exam for a paid bursary to George Heriot's, one of Edinburgh's oldest schools. For the sake of keeping the peace, I went through the motions. I wanted to go to a secondary school where I would know people and I had seen, in my mother, the product of a private education. I didn't want to end up the same. I was careful not to verbalise this, as it wasn't worth fighting about, and so I went along to Heriot's on a cold Friday morning with the intention of deliberately failing the exam. Although I was bright enough to pass the thing, I made a mess of it as a protest against the way I felt I was being treated. I set out with the sole intention of humiliating her as she had me many times in her life.

Although I achieved my aim of glorious failure, my plan backfired. My mum was able to turn the whole thing on its head when the results came through. While I lied about trying my best, she knew better. Over the next few days, she told anyone who would listen that I had turned down a place at Heriot's, implying that I had been successful in the exam and then exercised my right to choose otherwise. It made her out to be a really progressive, liberal mum with a highly intelligent son of whom she was incredibly proud.

I would learn the art of manipulation from her well as I grew into my teenage years and beyond. One face in public, another in private.

When I reflect upon those years now, I honestly cannot remember a time when my mother and I shared any loving moments. There was very rarely any calm and life was dominated by a constant anxiety, both of us bouncing off one another in a series of abusive outbursts. I did love her, I always have and always will, but when I was younger, respect for my mum was thin on the ground. The chaos we lived in prevented anything good from flourishing. I resented her many attempts to control me or bully me into submission but now I realise that she was simply way out of her depth. In my first decade, I wasn't mature enough to see and evaluate what was happening around me and I had begun to make disastrous choices off my own bat.

My perception hadn't developed sufficiently to see what a blind man could see: on a number of levels, my mum needed help. She never did get it but, like me, she worked it out all by herself and for that, in my book, she is deserving of the utmost admiration and respect.

9

Money

1980

There would still be the odd slap now and again from my mum, just as a reminder that the power would always be there, but it was time for some changes. Around this point, I moved in permanently with my grandad: just up the stair from my mum but a million miles away from the hovel I had been raised in. Money was still tight but at least I had found a place of safety. I still had daily contact with Mum but to all intents and purposes I lived 'up the stair', 'in the room'.

I'd been at secondary school for a year or so before moving and, while my behaviour had begun to suggest otherwise, I really enjoyed being at the big school. I must have been the source of a great deal of frustration for many of the staff. Obviously intelligent (but not spectacularly so), I was more interested in being disruptive without actually going too far.

I was still dressed in mainly second-hand cast-offs and so my disruptive behaviour was designed to divert attention away from my scruffy, dirty, unkempt appearance; sadly, I was five years too young to immerse myself in the Punk Rock movement, which would have suited me perfectly. It was also around this time that I started smoking, drinking and stealing. I stole from my mum's purse and my grandad's

46

pockets. I stole from my friends' parents and my parent's friends. I stole from neighbours. In fact, if there was money to be taken, I stole it with absolutely no sense of guilt or remorse. I had no money and they had lots, as far as I could see, so I managed to persuade myself that it was fine to take some.

Even those who employed me from then on were not immune from my light-fingered activities; in fact, over time, it would be employers who provided me with the richest pickings of all. I had my first Saturday job at this time with Brown's electronics shop on George IV Bridge and I grew into a thief quickly – a very good one. I abused the trust of lots of people, many of whom had shown me nothing but kindness and compassion.

I would often hang about the local streets waiting for elderly neighbours. Using the pretext of being a nice helpful laddie, I would offer to take their bags of messages to their front doors. As soon as I had the bags in my hands, I'd march on ahead and, once at their doors, I'd check that I had ample time to dip the purse, replace it and nonchalantly sit at their doorstep, guarding the messages until the old lady caught me up. I'd leave them to take their bags inside, departing with a benevolent, self-satisfied grin after steadfastly refusing to accept any reward for my efforts. Money was everything to me and I cared not a jot how I procured it. Now those memories sicken me to the core.

My criminal activities were not just confined to theft. In my mum's house, I would vandalise a lot of her ornaments, trinkets and furniture. I would often scratch a distinctive star shape into wooden sideboards, wardrobes, tables and doors. It was my signature. If I couldn't sell it, I would break it, and if I couldn't break it, I would desecrate it. It always made me feel better at the time. I had found a way to hurt back and it was exhilarating.

During one of these acts, purely by accident, I discovered the satisfying consequences of self-harm. Out of chaos came catharsis when during yet another Sunday battle with my mum I deliberately put my fist through the glass panel of the toilet door. There was blood pouring from my ripped knuckles and hostilities were put on hold as I went alone, on foot, and presented myself at the Royal Infirmary's A&E

department. When I got there, I found myself actually enjoying the experience and the sting of the cuts paled into insignificance when I received the attention and sympathy of the nurses who tended to my self-inflicted injuries.

It continued when I went to school the following morning with my hand dramatically bandaged. The teachers went out of their way to be nice to me. My peers were fascinated by the sight of my purple-black coloured fingers held together with thick blue cat-gut stitches. I was the centre of everybody's attention for a wee while and I loved it.

From pain came a pleasure of the most delicious nature. I was a somebody.

I wanted more.

Over the next few years, I would occasionally harm myself but never regularly enough to create a pattern that would be obvious. On the one hand, I knew I would be looked on as a nutcase, a label I could well do without, and yet, on the other, the attention I craved was becoming more and more addictive. All I was doing was bringing my body into line with the rest of my life. The physical injuries became, to me, an expression of what was happening inside my mind. I was hurting but nobody could see that pain. The solution was to create a visible injury so that people could see for themselves just how much internal pain I was in. For me, self-harming was never a case of opening up my flesh in order to release the torment within and offer it a means of escape. I got no actual pleasure from the functional act of cutting myself or inflicting any other sort of pain. It was the result of my self-mutilation that gave me satisfaction. Pain has never been attractive to me: it was nothing more than the means to a sinister, fucked-up end.

Now into my second year at secondary school, I had an art teacher who was an oddball. She dressed strangely, spoke in riddles and was an ideal target for my classroom disruption. A mutual dislike developed rapidly. In those days, educational discipline was meted out regularly by teachers who were at liberty to use whatever means they saw fit, violent or otherwise. My art teacher leathered me across the face with the palm of her hand one day. I wasn't the first to be treated like this but I was definitely the first to retaliate in such an extreme way. I shrugged my shoulders and returned to my desk, waiting for the end of the lesson. She had declared war.

When the bell rang for lunchtime, I occupied myself by staring into my schoolbag until the rest of the class left the room. As I passed the teacher on the way to the door, I looked her directly in the eye and hissed out in a low whisper, 'You'll be fucking sorry, Miss. I'll make your fucking life a misery.' I walked out, completely uninterested in her demands for me to come back here NOW!

Another teacher had given me six of the best fairly recently with a three-pronged tan-coloured leather tawse. By the time of the incident with the art teacher, this item was in my custody, safely hidden in my grandad's linen cupboard. I'd broken into the classroom in the dead of night and stolen the offending article from her drawer. No way was she going to get the better of me and the art teacher would get similar treatment, equally personal but much more impressive.

That lunchtime, I walked around the school building and hid amongst the rocks in the field outside the art teacher's classroom. I waited until the lights in the room went on, using the time to collect a pile of small hand-sized mini-boulders. I gave her enough time to settle into her packed lunch and a false sense of security before throwing a succession of the stones through the windows I knew to be closest to her desk, showering her with a thousand tiny shards of glass. Quickly, I then ran across the very familiar terrain, climbed over a wall into Holyrood Park and turned along the path that led back to my mum's, where I spent the rest of the lunch hour. I had got my revenge and as far as I was concerned that should have been the end of it.

When I returned to the art class the following week, I was astounded to observe the odd sight that greeted me, as was the rest of the class. My efforts at vandalism had been the talk of the school for a few days but the subject had died a natural death and nobody was any the wiser as to my involvement. We all stood agog, staring at the row of windows before us, as on every individual pane of glass (around 16 in each frame) had been put a cross of thick beige masking tape. As the class settled down, the teacher looked directly at me as she launched into a rousing evangelical tirade of warning directed at anyone who would dare break 'the cross of Jesus'. She had obviously lost it. It was magnificent. I had really got to her and now she was throwing down the gauntlet, throwing the ball back into my court.

Because I lived in such close proximity to the school, I was in no hurry to carry out my plans. I'd happily wait until the original window-breaking incident was nothing more than a distant memory. Then, late one night, along with a couple of local lads, I stole stealthily through the moonlight into the small field outside the art classroom, where the stations of the cross were still in place in the windows. There, I found the large pile of rocks I had been stockpiling. Enthusiastically, we executed our task, the noise of stone on glass shattering the silence in the cool night air until every last 'cross of Jesus' was destroyed. With no reason to linger, we went our separate ways and within minutes I was safely tucked up in my bed. We had taken out around 200 panes of glass and the whole manoeuvre had taken less than five minutes from start to finish. I fell asleep quickly, looking forward with great delight to going to school the following morning. Double art – I couldn't wait.

Halfway through the lesson, I was sent for by the headmaster. Waiting for me was my mum, who had been asked to come across the road to attend a meeting concerning 'a very serious matter'. When accused of the vandalism to the art room (now boarded up and in the relative dark), I held my nerve and denied everything, even when threatened with the police. They both knew that I was responsible for causing the damage but I knew they couldn't prove it. That was good enough for me. When the glass was eventually replaced in the windows, up went the sticky-tape crosses yet again. It was boring by then and they remained intact until the building was redeveloped a few years later. I moved on to other things. The broken windows were just my way of making a statement that I would not be fucked around with. I was able to let go after doing what I had to do. I had made my point.

10

Love

1982–83

In the summer of 1982, a school trip to Barra was planned. I had high hopes about how I'd spend my time, as I had developed my first real crush. Kaighlee was also going on the trip and I fantasised about sweeping her off her feet in the most romantic ways my 13-year-old mind could dream up. I pictured us walking hand-in-hand along the seafront, wearing the football shirts of the respective teams we supported. I had even taken to attending the home matches of her team, my deadly rivals, just to catch a glimpse of her as she stood with her dad in the family enclosure. That was dedication. I was besotted with her but, as would be the case throughout my life with most of my hopeful infatuations, it came to nothing. She was beautiful – I wasn't. She came from money – I didn't. She was clean and well groomed – I was grubby and unkempt. She was stable and undamaged – I was a fuck-up with a weird mum. No way would she give me even a first look, never mind a second one.

The trip to Barra was not a complete washout, however, as that is where I had my first proper kiss, during a World Cup match that was playing away on the telly in the room where someone suggested a game of spin the bottle. There were three girls, all from higher years, and three boys including myself. I remember experiencing a feeling of dread mixed with excitement when the bottle finally pointed towards me and I was going to get to kiss a real girl. The bottle was spun again, this time by me to choose just who would be the lucky lady. All that really remains clear to me is that after snogging away with this lassie, she broke off quite abruptly and gave me a condescending row for being too 'rough'. Always one to listen to those more experienced than me, I took the advice on board during my second attempt, which was with the next girl, and my efforts were much improved. This snogging lark was easy!

The trip itself was great. I had never felt so at ease with myself and my surroundings as I did during that week. We were given the freedom to organise our own days and the time went far too quickly. Most of the time, I chose to wander along to the ferry pier at Castlebay and sit, quite happy, reading a book in the raw June sunshine or simply staring over the sea in the direction of the castle that stood alone on a smaller island. I was a different person in that place with no fear, no angst and no hatred. But like all good things, the trip ended too quickly. On the ferry, as the seascape became landscape and then cityscape, my mood darkened, as I knew that I was returning to misery, conflict and violence. There was nothing whatsoever I could do about it.

After a summer of constantly avoiding my mum and her increasingly unpredictable manic outbursts, it was back to school, this time into the third year, which meant a change of location. The senior school was a mile or so away and I had to break my habit of crawling out of my pit when I heard the first bell from the school across the road.

At this point, I had been a member of the Boys' Brigade for a few years and while in the past it had just been somewhere to go to escape the madness of home for a few hours, I started to take the activities and ethos of the BB quite seriously. And it was the BB that gave me a taste of performing in front of a huge crowd, resulting in what was an absolutely terrific buzz.

I responded well to the BB philosophy of discipline, particularly the wearing of a highly polished uniform in which I took obsessive pride. The captain, a man named Alec Robertson, was one of life's good guys, who gave up a lot of his free time for the Company. It was Mr Robertson who encouraged me to enter the annual inter-Company Bible-reading competition, open to all boys from the Edinburgh and Leith areas, when I was 14 – and I actually won the thing! The Bible, and religion in general, meant very little to me but from the way I read aloud at BB headquarters in Victoria Street that evening I could have been mistaken for the Moderator of the Church of Scotland. Winning that competition opened up opportunities. I was invited to do a reading at Meadowbank Stadium as part of the BB Centenary service to be held for the whole of the Lothian membership. On the October day of the service, I was on a podium, alongside a minister and another boy, right in the middle of the arena, facing the vast imposing stand. Company by Company, thousands of boys marched in through the large royal-blue steel gates. The whole parade took over an hour to arrive.

When it was time for me to deliver my reading, I was shaking as I approached the lectern. With thousands of pairs of eyes and quite a few television cameras upon me, I took a deep breath, looked up and began to speak. I shut out the sound of myself echoing all around and settled to deliver a flawless reading. As I sat down, I was exhilarated: I had done something very few people would ever do; in fact, when I thought about it, there could only ever be one Centenary and I had been a central figure in the proceedings. I was walking on air as I left the stadium.

By now (after paying attention in biology, although it had taken a severe knuckle-rapping with a ruler to cause me to be more attentive), I had worked out that my mum suffered from pre-menstrual tension and so I had resolved to keep well out of her way when the madness was due. I was sleeping at my grandad's and spending most of my time there but, naturally, I did see a lot of my mum and tended to be in and out of that house frequently, too. She would insult me with ease for the slightest misdemeanour, although by this time I was instigating a lot of the strife myself. I'd begun, perversely, to enjoy the sheer sport of it. I'd occasionally retaliate with words but it would be a while before I was in my mother's league and so I'd antagonise her physically as well. It would be a rare occasion for me to actually strike my mum but I would regularly lash out at her belongings without a care in the world.

I also had a few quid of my own in my pocket from my Saturday job at the electrical shop, earning £5 a day and thieving up to ten times that much. My appearance had improved, as I got into buying my own clothes, and with this came a bit of a swagger. I had always looked older than my age and it was a natural thing for me to involve myself in Scotland's national sport – drinking. While I always hated the actual taste of alcohol, drinking it came fairly easily. While in the pub with friends, I would down pints in one go and chase with whatever spirit happened to be there. I enjoyed getting pissed, as it took me away from myself. Drinking to excess was just one way I found of running away from things, and to hell with the consequences. Strangely, my mum (a non-smoking teetotaller) was reasonably calm about my drinking – there was, however, one drink-related incident that would raise her hackles significantly higher.

It was Christmas Eve, 1983, a week before my 15th birthday, and I'd gone out for the afternoon with some other under-age wasters from school with the intention of getting absolutely guttered. Suited and booted, we had planned to make a night of it but unfortunately I, the one who usually got served alcohol anywhere, was refused entry to a nightclub that we normally got into without any problem. Seeing no point in arguing with the bouncers, I moved along with another faceless lad and found a pub in a backstreet just off the Royal Mile. At closing time, we staggered across the road into a chip shop, where I held on grimly to the counter, swaying and staggering. At one point, a girl in the queue said to me, 'If you can stand up on your own for ten seconds, I'm yours for the night.' Merry Christmas to me, I thought, as I lifted my hands from the counter. Before the stopwatch got anywhere near ten seconds, I was slumped in a heap, face down on the deck. And that really should have been the unceremonious end to a very drunken day out. It turned out to be just the beginning.

I have absolutely no idea how I got back home but I found myself banging on the back door of my mother's house, demanding to be let in. The door remained firmly shut. I ran round to the front door, kicked it in and stormed into the house. I scattered everything in my path, leaving a trail of destruction, until there I was in the kitchen, face to face with my mum, my tormentor-in-chief. We traded nasty, cruel and vindictive insults. I was looking to hurt her as deeply as possible. She wouldn't back down an inch, which enraged me further.

As she screamed at me, I leaned backwards with violent purpose and then smashed my forehead into her face. Blood spurted instantly from her burst nose. I pulled back my clenched fist, intending to assault my mother further, and at that vital moment, the point of no return, I felt a dull, heavy ache crawl over the top of my head, stopping me in my tracks and dazing me. Lucy had battered me over the head with a steel breadbin lid and my skull had connected with the rim. Now blood poured down my face and mingled with the outpourings from my mother's nose.

At that moment, I sobered up and saw clearly just what I had become. After years of loneliness, rejection and brutality, I had turned into the uncaring bastard I believed my absent dad to be and the aggressive bully my mum had become in order to survive.

I was an unholy mix of the two and I despised myself. I was empty, loveless and alone. How far would I go in the future? If my sister hadn't intervened, I am certain I would have killed my mother that Christmas Eve. What made it even worse was that in the immediate aftermath I felt not the slightest hint of remorse.

When I came to my senses, I fled back around the corner and climbed the drainpipe from which I could access my grandad's house. As I stood, wobbling on the windowsill, adrenaline still pumping through my body and screaming yet more obscenities to the world, Grandad finally opened the window and dragged me inside. He lifted my blood-soaked form into his arms the way a parent holds a newborn and kept me close until I fell into a very fitful sleep. My grandad knew all about the effects of drink and he would never mention what happened that night.

I awoke the next morning in a room that Santa had forgotten to visit during the night. I was in my single bed and I felt ill. Slowly, the events of the previous night came back to me as I tried to run my fingers through my matted hair. I was still a kid but I had almost killed my mother. Stale alcohol leaked from my pores. Raw vomit lay suspended in folds in my bed cover. I was surprised to see that I was still fully dressed – suit, tie, shoes, the lot. I could feel an enormous lump on the top of my head and I knew I would have to get my arse up to the hospital to have the cut stitched. My knuckles were skinned and swollen. I looked in the mirror. The teenage laddie staring back at me was an even uglier, monstrous caricature of myself. My once-white shirt was covered in blood, and vomit encrusted my crumpled grey suit jacket.

I was a fucking mess.

11

[In]Famous

1984–85

That performance brought the curtain down on what had been an awful year. My relationship with my mum had all but disintegrated and there was no way I could justify what I'd turned into. I had brought a lot of it on myself but, while I'd grown up fast, I was still a vulnerable child in a lot of ways. Without the security and routine of school, I know I would have drifted into decline a lot further than I actually did. It was a lifeline for me and I had already decided to stay on for as long as they would have me. After a severe talking- to about my attitude from my chemistry teacher, a man I respected greatly, I got my head down and started to behave. Almost overnight, I matured into a reasonably hard-working, interested student. I even unearthed hidden sporting talents and was first-choice goalkeeper for the school football team. The demons were never far from the surface, though.

I had got myself a job as a barman in a sleazy, downmarket go-go bar near to my school after I had ridiculously become a regular. In the year leading up to the Christmas Eve when I assaulted my mother, I was drinking heavily. I could be seen swigging from cans of export on the walk across the Meadows at half past eight in the morning as I went to school. Sometimes I would deliberately get pissed at lunchtime and then go to class.

My intoxication in school was noticed by the staff but instead of being heavy-handed with me, my chemistry teacher, Dr Gerry Carolan, got hold of me and talked some sense. In the deserted corridor outside his classroom, he obstructed my progress and went off on one, pointing out what my choices were doing, not only to me but to people like him who actually gave a fuck and couldn't stand back and watch me piss my potential up against the wall. I was under no illusions as to what I should do. At just turned 16, I stopped drinking and, after giving up my pub job, tried to keep away from drinking as a hobby. I knew that I was acting like an arsehole with alcohol and having someone I respected point it out to me was just what I needed.

Dr Carolan (or, as he was known, 'The Doc') hailed from Kilmarnock and was a very strong positive influence on me, even down to certain words that I still pronounce in the way he did, with his West Coast twang. It was the Doc who picked me to play for the school football team and eventually brought me on board to assist him with the Under-13s when I moved up a year. In the latter part of my school life, even when I had dropped chemistry, I always found him very approachable and light-hearted, and I'd lean on him whenever I felt I had a problem, not only with school but also with life. Never once did he send me away and I did appreciate that. He was one of the good guys and I have never had the opportunity to express my gratitude for his input during what was a very troubled time for me.

The drinking had been a useful smokescreen but now I became more obsessed with finding out as much as possible about my father. All the other male relatives I had could never quite satiate my craving to have my dad in my life. In order to locate him, I knew I would need money. That had been a strong motivating factor in terms of my choice to work at such a relatively young age. The bonus was that jobs also gave me plenty of opportunity for thieving as well and I had quite the talent for that.

I had been sacked from the electrical shop for stealing but moved on to find jobs in hotels, shops and as a labourer for a landscape gardener during the summer holidays, sometimes working in two or three places at a time. I earned quite decent money as a schoolboy but I also stole and scammed my way around until I was discovered and inevitably given the boot. Crucially, I was never prosecuted. I'd stopped stealing from my mum and grandad, although he would always blame me for thieving from his pockets on the mornings when he woke up skint after a serious session at the pub. As far as he was concerned, and rightly so, I was a dog with a bad name. At one time in my early teens, I'd attempted to defraud him of £300 by forging his signature on a bank withdrawal slip, which was noticed the next time he went to the bank himself. The police were initially involved but when I eventually owned up to the local beat cop, a good friend of the family, my grandad surprisingly agreed not to pursue the matter any further. He never got angry or violent with me over that and I respected him a damn sight more than I ever had because he was so decent about it. I think he understood why I had done it and he said that I could pay him back in instalments from whatever wages I earned in the future. I never did pay bit by bit. I worked hard, stole harder and gave him back £500 in one go. Patterns were beginning to emerge in my life and they would become more and more obvious as well as more and more damaging as the years progressed.

12

Strike

1985–86

In May 1985, at the end of my fifth year at high school, I passed my Highers. While my results weren't stunning, they were more than adequate, particularly in light of the fact that I never revised at all. In August, I started to make the most of my final year at school by achieving something that would have been unthinkable a few years earlier.

This was the year of a teachers' strike, which meant, most importantly of all, no football. With no staff available to involve themselves in extra-curricular activities, I decided to put the experience gained when assisting the Doc with the running of the Under-13s into practice for my own team. Only one problem stood in my way. The industrial action was not exclusive to our school, so that meant there was no one to play against. As I, along with the majority of my peers who supported the action taken by the teachers, thought about how to overcome this sporting dilemma, a plan began to germinate.

Together with a mate of mine, we decided to try to combine our need for a game of football with a chance to get the school some free publicity. We went down to Easter Road Stadium and asked if we could play Hibs' youth team in order to raise awareness of the teachers' dispute. With no one in their right mind in Scotland supportive of Margaret Thatcher, the coach agreed and fixed up the details there and then. The boys in our team, most of us Hibs fans, were made up, so training began in earnest for our big match. Next stop was the *Edinburgh Evening News*, who came and did a smashing article about the upcoming fixture, complete with a big half-page photo of me and my mate Sean in our football kits.

Come the day of the big match, to be played at our home ground just off Ferry Road, our dressing-room was buzzing. Half the school, pupils and striking teachers alike, had turned up to watch the match, as well as friends and relatives. As the boys got changed, I waited at the main gates of the ground to greet the arrival of the Hibs team.

And I waited.

And I waited.

The longer I stood there, the further my heart sank, as it dawned on me that they weren't coming. I felt bad enough for myself but ten times worse for the people who had come along to watch and at least a hundred times worse for the rest of the lads. Frantically, I tried to call Easter Road but the phone just rang out. A few of the lads had become understandably restless and so I had to face them all and tell them that there would be no proper game of football played that afternoon. After a half-hearted kick around, we all trudged home, bitterly disappointed.

The next morning, I woke up in my bed at Grandad's and the first thing I did was phone my contact at Hibs. I was fed a lot of nonsense about them trying to call the school to say they were unable to fulfil the obligation they had made to us. I told the guy that I didn't believe him and that a lot of people had been disappointed. He said something non-committal about getting back in touch at a later time and hung up. I went back to my bed, as I wasn't due in school until later in the morning. Just as I had dozed off, I was roused back into life by my grandad's Bakelite phone. It was the reporter from the *Evening News* looking to see how the match had gone. I had clean forgotten about the paper's interest. Wide awake, within seconds I saw a chance to salvage something from the disaster and that night, 25 September 1985, on the front page was the headline – 'Hibs let us down say boys' team'. I was quoted several times, the most memorable of which was the line: 'They have offered us a re-match but we'll really have to think hard about that.' The morning after the article appeared in the paper, a lot of teachers said how well I'd handled the situation and that some of their teacher mates (teachers had mates?) from other schools had been in touch, all expressing admiration at the positive publicity the school had received.

That, I suppose, should really have been the end of it but, buoyed by the sudden upturn of events, after school Sean and I jumped on a number 2 bus and headed west – destination Tynecastle, home to Hearts FC, local rivals to Hibs. After presenting ourselves at the main reception, we were ushered into the manager's office, where the youth-team coach, Walter Borthwick, was sat on the edge of a huge desk, smiling benevolently. Obviously he had seen the stuff in the paper and wryly said, before we could get a word in, 'You should have come to us first, we've been expecting you, and before you ask, the answer's yes. How does next Thursday, three o'clock at your place, sound? We'll get a ref sorted, if that's OK.' Sean and I were delighted. We would get our game against a big team after all.

The team was even more enthusiastic when the match kicked off and we even surprised ourselves by holding Hearts for 35 minutes. After they got their first goal through a penalty, we lost our discipline, caved in and took a lesson from the pros. We eventually lost 16 (yes, 16) –0. We had achieved something pretty unique and even after such a severe hammering we went out and partied well into the night as only 16-year-old lads can.

The football-team success was the ideal platform from which I would launch my campaign to achieve what I would never have thought was within my grasp. Just to prove that I could, I threw my proverbial hat into the ring to be nominated as head boy in October 1985. Unbelievably, I was elected comfortably by my year group after I stood up in front of them and gave a rousing 'bad boy made good' speech. Although I appeared to want it badly, being head boy was of little interest to me or my ego. It was the challenge that was important, the rising up from underdog status. The fact that I was the least likely candidate, probably in the school's history, made it something I pursued with a passion. I also have to admit that there was something about other people choosing me, *me*, that appealed to the needy side of my personality.

* * *

The day I left school in 1986 aged 17 was a sad one. My school life had expired naturally. Real life had never really been an appealing prospect, as I knew that I'd struggle to cope, and I also knew that school was good for me, given that I had structure and a purpose there. I left with no full-time job lined up, no university place and very little direction. Out of school, my life was again entering another stage of chaos. I was still living in my grandad's house but was pretty much self-reliant. With no one left to impress, I quickly slid into depression. I still argued constantly with my mum whenever our paths crossed and afterwards I would inevitably self-harm. I would cut my arms, smash windows with my fists or swallow huge amounts of tablets. At this time, it was not about attention, more to do with rejection and frustration and the need to feel loved.

But some things *were* about to change.

My appearance had improved, as I was now in total control of the contents of my wardrobe as well as being fastidiously clean and tidy. Four years earlier, I had met a girl called Catriona, who knew the girlfriend of my mate Alan, but she hadn't looked twice at me then. I'd changed a great deal physically since that time and she was now keen. Desperate to join the legions of the sexually competent, I began to spend some time with her. She and her sister lived in Glenrothes and, as Alan had passed his driving test, we spent a lot of time in his dad's car on journeys over the Forth Road Bridge. To be honest, looking back, while I appeared mature, I was nowhere near emotionally equipped to deal with even a casual relationship. I was too needy and before long I found myself becoming unhealthily obsessed with Catriona. Although I wasn't aware of it at the time, looking back on it, even at this early stage, the foundations for the future were determined, as the line that separated sex and love was already blurred in my mind.

During my last days at school, all my mates had been happily boasting about their sexual exploits but I was still a virgin, eagerly hoping for that all-important opportunity to present itself. I was willing to go with anyone who thought they might, on the off-chance, like to have sex with me. On 19 May 1986, aged 17 years and 149 days, the deed was finally done with Catriona in the romantic grounds of Fife Council HQ in Glenrothes. What a Casanova!

It wasn't long before I honestly started believing that I had fallen in love with Catriona. The reality was that I had become infatuated with her and thought about her obsessively whenever we were apart. I had arranged to meet her one night in a nightclub in Kirkcaldy and on my arrival I scanned the interior, looking for, as I now considered her to be, 'my girlfriend'. At first glance, I couldn't see her, so I got myself a pint. I saw her sister sitting in a corner bay staring into space, but no Catriona. I circled the place one more time before I approached her sister. Still nothing. Perhaps I had been stood up. I resigned myself to drinking up and going back home on the train, disappointed.

It was then that I noticed a couple, mouths entwined, limpet-like, sitting beside the sister. Of course, it was Catriona snogging another bloke. In an instant, I was furious. I ran to where they were sitting, prised their heads apart and punched the poor bemused guy flush on the nose, splitting it apart with a sickening squelching sound. I didn't wait for the approaching bouncers to grab me and throw me out. I just turned towards them, raising my hands in a placatory gesture, told them I was leaving anyway and went.

I wandered around the streets, feeling a knot squeezing me from inside. Jealousy mixed with rejection. I embraced this new type of pain. I was just about to take my first steps on the lonely journey of serious self-harm. Up until then, I had been playing at it. Now I was ready to make the statement of all statements. At least, I thought I was. It would actually take years of preparation and practice. But then, in that small town, in the middle of the night, the dummy run would feel like the real thing. What had happened with Catriona confirmed to me that I was a fat, ugly weirdo who wasn't worthy of love. Life was truly awful that night and I decided that I wanted to end it.

In the early hours of the morning, as I waited at Kirkcaldy Station for the first train back to Edinburgh, I climbed on top of the not-very-high station roof and made a token gesture of a suicide attempt. While it felt very real to me, it was with a slightly sprained ankle that I stepped back down from the top rung on the ladder of my personal discontent.

I'd learn.

13

Hurt

1986

Once I left school, I had no job and was just drifting around, disenfranchised and uninterested in pretty much everything. In the 1980s, jobs were like lottery wins and I was nobody's jackpot as an employee. My descent into serious self-harm accelerated over the next few months as the relationship with my mum continued to be fractious. Only sheer luck prevented me inflicting permanent damage on myself. I had graduated to razor blades, which actually felt good, almost comforting, on my skin before the cutting commenced. I initially scratched away at parts of my body that could be concealed underneath clothing. The cutting became more violent as the yearning I had for my father developed into an unhealthy obsession.

I'd inflicted superficial cuts to my wrists and some deeper ones to my chest and upper arms. I was hurting badly as I started to dwell on all the shitty things that life had thrown my way and I needed someone, anyone, to see my pain, acknowledge it and perhaps even take it away. I was in no fit state to function but still I maintained a 'normal' exterior in public. Only one former schoolfriend ever sussed what I was doing. I wish I'd listened to him when he told me to stop, told me to get help, but I didn't.

One Saturday night, before going out to a party, I opted to show the world just how much pain I was in. I got to my knees in my grandad's living room, closed my left eye and repeatedly smashed it against the brass doorknob. When I was satisfied with the bruising I had caused, I took a new razor blade and carefully sliced the swollen area just underneath my lower eyelid. When I checked over the damage in a mirror, I immediately felt better: my pain had been validated and I was satisfied that the results looked really worthy of sympathy and attention. Smacking my eye off a lump of solid brass seemed perfectly normal to me and the cut on the bone of the socket was just the flamboyant underscore. Here was something I could do well, something that had a purpose and an end product, but, most of all, something that, however temporarily, made me feel better.

The reaction from the people at the party was as predictable as it was brief. I think people knew that my tale of getting into a fight on the way down the road was bullshit but, because my injury had little impact on their own lives, they were happy to indulge me until their attention was diverted by more compelling people than the fuck-up with the black eye. I felt that I had to raise my game, up my performance with the blades, and when my eye had healed up, I progressed to the next level.

In the full knowledge that what I was about to do would result in hospital attention, I carefully wrapped a small length of tissue paper around one end of a fresh shiny razor blade to prevent any telltale nicks on my fingers. With my left hand holding the small vanity mirror recently acquired from my mother, I raised the cutting edge of the blade, gingerly held between my right thumb and forefinger, slowly towards my right cheek, lightly pushing it into the soft spongy flesh to get the feel of it. This required full and absolute concentration, and so it was without even the slightest hint of emotion that when the first minuscule spots of blood appeared at the razor's edge I tilted the blade in order to get the corner of it through the flesh and subsequently achieve the necessary purchase and pressure required to rip an inch-and-a-half-long opening in one methodically swift downward movement. The blood oozed from the gaping aperture that now dominated my ugly, deformed face. I had created what I saw as a ghastly, perverse work of art and, although it stung like hell, I gazed proudly into the mirror as I watched, entranced, the blood drip drip dripping onto the floor below.

I went up to the Royal Infirmary. After the care and diligence of the staff, whose time and talents I was abusing, I returned home to my grandad's feeling clean but not cleansed, sewn up but incomplete, shiny and new but damaged and fragile. Even now, looking back after 20 or so years, I have little understanding of what was going on in my head. I had become very focused on finding my dad and the longer he remained unfound, the more severe my self-inflicted damage became.

Things had happened to me but they had been either bottled up and hidden away or simply glossed over. I was a vulnerable and fragmented young man only months away from his 18th birthday. I was visibly crumbling but no one seemed to notice. I don't suggest, however, that there was anyone else to blame for the mess I had created – that's far too easy a cop-out – but there were things that contributed to and exacerbated my behaviour. All that mattered was the pain. My life was catching up with me and I felt powerless to deal with the fact that there was no escape. I would run from it as fast and for as long as I could. I would run until running was no longer an option but in the meantime I would run straight into something even worse.

14

Man

27–28 JANUARY 1987

I am alone. Alone but content. Occasionally I glance at the caged female gyrating in time to the music. I raise my glass to my mouth and slowly sip. I am not a stranger to places like this. Alcohol and I have been friends for years. I am sitting. Alone. Reading my paper. I am in a man's world and now I am a man. A real man. I enjoy this world. This is the world I have craved all my life.

The bar is almost empty and I enjoy the space. There is another man sitting in the corner across from me. He is also alone. He is a large man with a bushy moustache and thick black hair. He is a well-dressed man. He has money. I can't see it but I know he has it. I envy him. I wonder if he is a nice man. I turn back to the semi-naked woman in the cage. She is the only woman in the bar. In this man's world. She looks bored and is chewing a piece of gum. The nice man is standing beside me. He would like to read my paper; would I mind? He is a very polite man and his soft tones are at odds with his largeness. He sits down opposite me effortlessly and picks the newspaper up. As he reads it, I read him. He has chubby fingers and thick hairy wrists, which are exposed as his leather sleeves ride up.

He is talking to me. I am talking to him. This is what real men do.

We meet in pubs and we talk. We talk over glasses filled with brown or amber liquid; he tells me he is rich and I am impressed. Money impresses me greatly. It is the most important thing in the world to me. I want money. I want to be like him. Like the nice man. He tells me his name. I tell him mine. I do not lie. He asks what I do. I tell him I have no job. I tell him of my plans to work down south in a holiday camp sometime soon. I sent the form away only last week. He tells me he can help me. Perhaps. Am I interested? I nod.

He gets up from the table we now share and quickly returns with more brown liquid for me and an orange juice for him. He has a car. He has to pick up some girls shortly. Girls who are working. Working girls! Would I like to come along? I nod again. What harm can it do? He is a nice man and he will drive me home. He will tell me how to make lots of money. He has contacts in the holiday camp I have my heart set on. He will put in a good word for me. He is older, like a brother, maybe a father, and he makes me feel warm and safe.

A bell rings and we walk through the large, heavy wooden double doors into the late-night snow-covered street. The city looks beautiful. The snow has stopped falling and the air is crisp and clear. I love this city.

The nice man unlocks his car doors. It is a brown car. I get in. I am excited. I sense danger (he is a stranger) but I am no stranger to danger. No danger can come to me. I am a man. No danger. The car heads in the opposite direction from where I live. Of course. He has to pick the girls up first. The roads are empty. We stop at a large hotel and the nice man gets out and shuffles inside. I am alone. Alone in a cold brown car. I could get out and walk home. I don't. I stay in the car, as I am too lazy to walk. And a bit too drunk. The nice man dives out of the hotel. He is followed by two bottle-blonde women. They are wearing very short skirts and very high heels. They are not dressed for the weather. They are wearing their uniform. They have just finished working. Together. The taller woman is carrying a large black box and seems to be running towards the car. In her heels, in the snow. She almost slips but recovers in time.

The nice man is opening the hatchback of the car. I feel a rush of air on my neck as the taller woman places the black box carefully inside. The box is a television. It is quickly covered up with a blanket and the hatchback is slammed shut. The unlikely trio get into the car and it speeds away. The women are giggling, their half-exposed breasts jiggling up and down. Giggling and jiggling. The nice man shakes his head but has a benevolent expression on his face. The drink has taken effect and my head is spinning slightly. The car heads back across town and I am glad to be heading home. The women are still laughing, the sound punctuated only by high-pitched squeals and incessant chatter.

We park in a street I am not familiar with but feel I should be. I am invited into a large house. I follow the others inside. I am apprehensive but I have little will to protest. Anyway, I am a man. We climb some stairs and enter a large room. One of the unlikely trio flicks a switch and I shield my eyes against the shocking dark-pink decor.

My feet sink into the deep claret-coloured carpet. I see a bed. A large bed. I have never seen a bed as big as this before. There is a TV high on the wall, held in place with a bracket. There is a fridge in a corner. Everything else is pink. The bedclothes, the curtains, even the glasses on top of the bar (why is there a bar in here?).

I sit down on a pink sofa beside one of the women. I am handed a glass of something clear. I want it to be water. I drink it in one. It is not water. The women are still laughing. Why can't they shut up? My head feels fuzzy but not enough for me to pass out. I am slightly dizzy but I am aware of my surroundings (too much pink for me not to be).

The nice man is sprawled on top of the pink bed. The smaller woman with the larger breasts lies beside him. There is a hint of mischief in the air. I become excited but I do not show it. Maybe I will get to fuck one of the women. I am nervous. I have only ever fucked once before and that didn't go too well. I hope I don't embarrass myself when I get to do it.

I am given another drink and a big, fat, sweet-smelling roll-up to smoke. I am getting carried away with the moment and my own expectations. I am quivering with anticipation. I am going to fuck a woman. A real woman, not a skinny 16-year-old schoolgirl. I smoke the sweet roll-up and relax back into the soft pink sofa.

The woman beside me, the one I hope to fuck, gets up and walks slowly to the door. My eyes are fixed on her. The smaller woman straightens up from the bed she has been sharing with the nice man. I do not hear the door opening or closing but I know I am now alone on the sofa. Alone in the room with the nice man who still lies on the bed. With the women gone, the room is silent. The nice man presses a button and the TV on the bracket sparks into life, doing the same to me. There are images of naked people writhing around on a highly polished floor. They appear to be wet and I can't discern men from women. There is no sound coming from the TV. Instead there is music. Soft music. Soft music coming from a hi-fi hidden in a corner. I feel awkward, disorientated and disappointed. Disappointed as I know I will not be fucking that woman after all.

The man is talking to me. Talking about making money. Serious money. His face is somehow different from how I remember it. He asks me what I would do to make serious money. I say I don't know. He tells me tales of people who pay for sex. Businessmen with lots of money who are willing to pay high prices for the depraved acts he now describes. Depraved acts I don't fully understand. I tell him I am not interested. He says he knows a man who pays to watch someone fuck his wife. I shake my head. I stand up, my legs unsteady but capable. I say I must go. I must go home. I stagger and fall back onto the pink sofa.

The man removes his shirt. He has a blue cord hanging from his neck with a small key attached to it. He tells me I could make a lot of money just by dancing. He obviously hasn't seen me dance. He asks me to dance in front of him. Dance like the woman in the cage back in the bar we left in a different lifetime. I half snigger, half sneer at him. I have to get away but my legs are filled with jelly and my head spins even faster than before. The man lifts the blue cord with the key attached over his head. The music plays on and the naked bodies are still squirming across the polished floor.

The man puts the key into the top drawer in the bedside cabinet. He opens the drawer and lifts out a metallic black L-shaped object. It takes me a few seconds to see what the object is. I have never seen a real gun before. Jesus fucking Christ, what the fuck is going on here? I think I must be dreaming. I am having a nightmare and I will wake up soon. Soon, in my dream, I will be dead and then I will awaken. The man is going to shoot me.

Don't go with strangers. My mum always told me.

The man points the weapon at me. I can't take my eyes off it. 'Dance,' he says.

I dance. As I dance, I slowly remove my clothes. I am sexually inexperienced but I know what the man wants. I will give the performance of my life if I have to. The gun follows my deliberate movements as I use the floor as best I can. I am trying to remember how the caged women move when they do this. The man's free hand rubs his crotch through his trousers. I am now naked. He tells me what to do. I do what I am told. I am terrified; I have never known fear like this. I am disgusted and ashamed and I am naked, but still I dance, doing what I am told. The man choreographs me through a diabolic routine that strips me of everything. I hold myself apart for him to see. I am exposed. I am raw. I want to go home. I want to be anywhere but here. The music stops. I think it's all over. Will he shoot me or can I go?

Neither.

He still has a salacious grin across his large face. He unbuckles his belt with one hand and undoes his trousers. He releases his horrible swollen penis. It is the only erect penis I have ever seen apart from my own. It is ugly. It is angry. It is in front of me. The man soaks his awful appendage in transparent oil. He grabs my hand and guides it onto his cock. I feel a mixture of fear and revulsion. The gun is aimed at my chest. He demands I massage his cock. I do what I am told. I try to detach from what I am doing but I cannot. How the fuck did I get into this mess? My head is spinning. It spins with fear, not alcohol or drugs. I am sober now, very sober, and the nightmare is all too real. I am too sober. I pump away dispassionately. The man groans but does not come. He squeezes my wrist and tells me to stop.

After a few moments, he tells me to go down. I haven't a clue what he means but I move to lie down on the floor. Down on the floor. Down. The man is irritated. 'No,' he says, 'suck my cock!' Oh fuck, no, I think. I can't fucking do this. The cold steel pushed into my flesh convinces me otherwise. I allow my lips to part and his cock slides into my mouth. I am moving my head up and down, up and down, with his fetid member assaulting my tongue, my gums, my cheeks and my throat. I gag several times but the man doesn't seem to notice. I hope he doesn't come in my mouth. I will vomit. I know I will.

He doesn't come in my mouth.

He withdraws his cock and pushes my head to one side as he removes his jeans and pants. He leaves his grey socks on and I suppress a sudden nervous urge to laugh. Now he is naked, too, and I see he really is a large man. A big fat man. He tells me to lie face down on the bed as he rubs more oil into his cock. I think I know what's coming. I do what he says. I feel a cold viscous liquid snaking its way down the crack of my arse. The gun is pressed into the back of my head as I am slowly encased in hot, sticky, sweaty, acrid-smelling flesh.

I feel something probing near my anus. He has a finger inside me. It is unpleasant and uncomfortable but I stay silent. Another of his fingers enters me. He is moving his fingers in and out. I am motionless. I am sore and so, so scared. Still he works his fingers inside my arse, slowly trying to enlarge the tight space within me. I feel the heel of his hand brush against my arse cheeks with increasingly urgent frequency. Every muscle in my body is taut. He tells me to relax. I can't. I notice that the pillow my face is crushed into is damp with my sweat and tears. I notice I am sobbing. He removes his fingers. Perhaps he knows he has gone too far.

Perhaps not.

I feel a hot agony tearing through my whole being as my rectum is invaded by something far too large to belong there. It moves quickly. Up and down. In and out. It's sore. Why can't this be over? I think I would rather die than do this any longer. I am broken. I don't care for anything any more. I have been violated beyond anything I could ever imagine. Scraped out. In and out. Up and down. I hear the man's breathing increase and he emits a long deep groan.

And then.

And then nothing.

For a few minutes, he lies on top of me, kissing my neck in a parody of consensual tenderness while he gets his breath back. I am lying. Lying broken, face down on the hideous pink sheets. I am fucked. Literally fucked. I am sore inside and I want to die. I let this happen. I did nothing to stop it. I am a coward.

The man has dressed and he tells me to do the same. I get to my feet on very unsteady legs. An evil brew of fluids drips from between my legs, smearing pink onto the inside of my thighs. I dress quickly. I am staring at the gun again. With a glint in his eye, the man dramatically raises the weapon. I am cowering. I am crying. He is sniggering. He thinks this is funny. He pulls the trigger. Instinctively, I tense and recoil. I hear a dull click but it doesn't register. I look at the bad man. He is laughing heartily. The laugh is from the pit of his vermin-infested stomach. He throws the gun to the floor. It is a toy, a fake. 'It's a replica,' he roars through his laughter.

I hate him. Only a few hours before I had never met this monster and now I hate him.

I hate him.

I hate me.

I hate.

He is writing something on a piece of paper. He is opening the top drawer of the bedside cabinet again. He pulls out a wad of cash and pushes it, along with the piece of paper, into my hand. He closes my fist over the money. Serious money, he says, plenty more where that came from. He tells me to phone him if I want to make more money. I say I will think about it. I turn silently and walk out into the street. I do know this street. I had a school friend who lived here. I feel a dull throb behind my groin and my arse is on fire. I can't get this acrid, noxious taste out of my mouth, out of my mind.

The snow has become a dirty grey slush, the city now awash with muck. My city: filthy and dangerous. In this city, I have been raped. I hate this city. It is an ugly city. I throw the paper and the money into the air and the wind catches it and scatters it in all directions. Money is not important. Money is evil. Money is nothing.

I am walking towards my grandad's house but I know he is not there and so I can be alone. I have a key. I need to be alone. I need to be safe. What has just happened never happened. I am not queer. I am not homosexual. I am not a real man. I am not a man.

I am a boy and I have been damaged by a bad man in a man's world. Nobody will ever know. It is my sordid secret and I will not think about it ever again.

It never happened.

15

Daisy and Ray

1987

Repressed memory was something I considered to be nothing more than psychobabble. I couldn't accept that people with issues or psychological problems could in some way 'unremember' events that had happened to them, no matter how damaging or traumatic they were. This wasn't a view I reached in hindsight, years later, when I looked back on the life I had lived so far. I wasn't stupid, I was reasonably well informed, and during the 1980s there was a lot of coverage of issues concerning abuse and violence. I soaked it all up – and spat most of it out again. Unbeknown to me, however, as I opened a letter from England, I was subconsciously doing just what I thought was nonsense. With the distraction that this letter would provide, I was attempting to wipe out a memory that was so horrific, so destructive, but so very real that shutting it away and placing it in a sealed vault in the darkest recesses of my mind was the only way to cope. It would be seven years before I would face the contents of the vault, when an innocuous comment would open it. In the meantime, the memory would chip away inside of me, compounding the already significant damage. In the immediate wake of the vault being slammed shut, I was unsure as to why the particular need I had cultivated throughout my life thus far grew out of all proportion but what I did know was that I needed my dad. I needed him badly.

I had initiated tenuous enquiries with several agencies in the English counties nearest to where I believed my paternal grandparents were last known to reside in an attempt to finally locate Ray, my dad. One of those agencies was the Post Office and I received an official-looking envelope (sent to Grandad's address in order not to alert my mum) that contained a cutting from a free local advertising newspaper announcing the Ruby wedding celebrations of a Mr and Mrs Randall. Never having seen my father's parents, the photograph was of little value to me but, crucially, the accompanying article contained an address. There was also an unsigned Royal Mail compliments slip on which was handwritten, in blue ink, the words 'good luck'. I considered it a gamble worth taking.

Disorientated, jobless and drifting aimlessly with a faint hope of working in a holiday camp far away from my home, armed with the letter containing my dad's parents' details, I took myself in the direction of Middle England.

With a return ticket and £10 in my pocket, I boarded the train south from Waverley Station on a very cold, damp night in the early part of February 1987. As I took my seat on the train, my heart was beating hard; the time was right, I felt, to seek out the answers I believed I needed to make me whole.

The long overnight journey passed in the blink of an eye, as I spent the whole time fantasising about the adventure ahead of me. I was certain that I would find my father even though I only had his parents' address. My fantasies grew as I dreamed of an emotional reunion, with him declaring undying love for me and promising to make it all better. At other times, I envisaged me smacking him in the mouth as payback for his desertion.

I was on the platform of the railway station 300 miles away from home at around 7 a.m. After checking the address I had against a nearby wall map, I headed off in the direction of my 'other' grandparents' house. I was nervous, for sure, but I'd made it this far and there was no turning back. As I approached the front door, my calm exterior hid a frightened, quivering wreck. I was a wee boy all over again. This was it. I was going to meet my dad – a man I wouldn't even recognise if I walked past him on the street but a man I needed so, so badly.

I felt overcome with nausea. I couldn't go through with it. I turned away and found myself alone, sitting on a swing in a nearby play park. I sat for at least an hour debating with myself. Eventually, I reasoned that, having come this far, I had to follow the whole thing through. I went back and hammered on the door as if my life depended on it.

A small, obese, white-haired, elderly-looking woman came to the door and, without saying a word, burst into floods of tears, as I, the ghost of her eldest son, stood before her. No wonder I had not developed into one of the beautiful people. If I was looking at my dad's mother, then it made the way I looked suddenly obvious. It appeared that I shared a gene pool with this odd-looking woman who had so obviously climbed down, bashing her face on the way, from the ugly tree two generations previously. With a squat body as wide as it was long, and a squished-up bright-red face, this was no classical beauty. Her eyes darted nervously from behind two scar-like slits above her vein-cracked cheeks. Dressed in a huge, shapeless floral-patterned smock, thick, ruddy, corned-beef arms complete with bingo wings wobbled away. The smock stopped just below the knees to make way for a pair of elephantine nylon-clad ankles attached to feet squeezed into pink elasticated slippers.

This was, indeed, the woman who was my other 'granny', and what a contrast to the real grandmother I had lost 11 years before. Daisy was the diametric opposite to Annie. They were worlds apart. Daisy, with a lumbering waddle and a filthy tongue (the first thing I had heard her say was 'Faaarking 'ell' in a grating London accent), was as unappealing as Annie had been attractive.

Daisy clucked and fussed as she ushered me through to the large kitchen situated at the back of the semi-detached cottage she had lived in most of her life. I was nervous, chain-smoking and not saying very much, but I managed to bring myself back to my senses and turned on the charm. My sole thought, inexplicably, was to remain loyal to my mum and not let her down. I decided that I would be a credit to her and not show her up. It was as much a tribute to my real granny's memory that I lied and blustered on about what a great life I had and how happy I was to live it. Time to put on another show.

While it should have been more than evident just by looking at Daisy that her drug of choice would be of the eaten variety, I was still surprised when a mountain consisting of more fried food than I had ever seen in one place at one time was put down on a plate in front of me. 'You must be farking starving,' Daisy said. 'Get that darn you.' As I toyed with the grease-saturated meat mountain, I overheard Daisy speaking on the phone in what was plainly her 'posh voice'. I heard her say, 'Ray? You better get raand, Jiffrey's 'ere.'

My father, Ray Randall; Ray (I would never call him Dad to his face) worked and lived locally after travelling extensively for most of his life. (I always wondered, though never asked, just what it was that *he* was running away from.) After half an hour or so, I heard a key slide into the front door. This was it. I was only seconds away from coming face to face with the man I had elevated to mythical status: the man I had always hoped would be my salvation and would surely, just by his very presence, mend the many flaws in me. The only man in the world I so desperately wanted to love me, to take me in his arms and tell me everything would be OK.

My dad.

MY DAD!

The tears that lurked just behind my eyes were sucked back in. I had to work very hard not to explode. Into the kitchen came a small, fat, baldy, bearded man in a grey suit, who casually walked towards me with a very distinctive, very familiar 'pigeon-toed' gait. Now I knew why I had a funny walk that had been the subject of much teasing and derision during my schooldays.

I stood up from the table and extended my right arm. He took my hand in a weak grip. I simply said, 'All right, Ray?' as I battled not to betray my real feelings.

I spent the next week in the company of my father, meeting his (my) family, and slowly I learned of a past that, with some clever editing, presented the package of my father in a much more favourable light

79

than I had ever imagined possible. He admitted affairs and his inability to cope as a parent. But when he showed me the names of the other woman's kids (not his) etched into his arm, close to a tattoo displaying his pet name for my mum, I baulked. There, I should have realised, was the truth of what my father thought of me. My absence from the list inked on his arm was an indication that I was insignificant. However, with my head full of need, I allowed myself to enjoy the time I spent with him, trying hard to impress him as I listened intently to a man I found to be charming, self-effacing and very funny. Over the course of the week, I devoured all information but when it was time to go I knew I'd learned nothing at all. I hadn't solved the mystery of myself. I was none the wiser as to why my life had taken the turns it had and why I still felt so fucking lost and empty.

I waved to him from the train. I'd found my father but I was more hollow and confused than ever before. Yes, I'd liked him – perhaps a bit too much – but as the week had unfolded I no longer wanted to be like him. When I thought about it on the journey back north, I contemplated just how crap a dad he really was. I wouldn't do what he had done. I'd be different. I would try to treat people with respect and dignity; I would honour the sanctity of marriage if I ever found someone who would choose to love me for the rest of their life. But most of all, I resolved, I would not be the kind of father he was. If the future held for me a life of parenthood, I would do the opposite of what he had done and be a good, loving, available dad. I hoped, though, that it wouldn't come to that, as I truly, passionately, even more so after meeting my own father, believed that I was safe in the knowledge that I never wanted any children. Not for me, thank you very much. I knew what was what.

I knew nothing.

16

Retribution

1987

I returned to Edinburgh and my grandad's, where I'd spend the next eight months. My mother was really upset that I'd gone to England behind her back and, after my trip down south, even although I was living just up the stair, we avoided each other whenever possible. Meeting my father was something that I had to do and while I recognised my mum's antipathy towards him, I felt, at the time, that she was being unfair. After all, she could never understand how it actually felt to be raised without a dad – she still had hers and had done all her life.

I returned with high hopes of developing my relationship with Ray but after a few letters, phone calls and a flying visit from him, contact dwindled. While it hurt for a while, I was used to coping without him, so, in reality, nothing was lost. I'd received a letter from the holiday camp I had applied to for employment but it remained unopened until I eventually ripped it up, unread, and threw it away. Having shut the experience of January away in the back of my mind, I felt that letter was contaminated and the optimism I had had when I had filled out the application had long since faded away.

I was jobless, penniless, friendless and drifting. I wanted a regular job, a social life and, most of all, a proper girlfriend, someone to be close

81

to. I dreamt of marriage, a big house, fancy car – but definitely no kids. My dreams were dissolved by reality, as I knew that I was a fat, ugly freak. It was better to remain alone than be rejected and disappointed. It was safer to share a house with an elderly man than go out and get a proper life of my own.

My grandad awoke one Saturday morning with what must have been the deadliest of hangovers, having been out on the lash for two days solid. Grandad was, even in his later years, a very capable and adept fighter. A strong man, with huge hands and a toned heavyweight boxer's physique, he was a seriously formidable opponent. When I was 12, I remember seeing him batter several colours of shite out of two young men in their 20s who had been taking the piss. He left them sprawled on the pavement after grabbing their necks in either hand and crashing their foreheads together. Grandad just picked up his shopping bags and continued up the road, walking away as if nothing out of the ordinary had happened.

That particular morning, I was rudely awakened by him cursing, roaring and leathering me across my bare back with a walking stick as I lay face down in my single bed. Initially disorientated, I squirmed away from the blows, then jumped to my feet and asked him what the fuck was going on. He shouted that I was all the thieving bastards of the day and wanted to know where the money I had taken from his pocket was. Instantly, I knew that he had spent the lot in the pub but he was beyond the point of reason. He had even slept in the trousers that I had supposedly dipped but it didn't matter to him. I had stolen from him before, so that was it – I was guilty. As I stood facing him, defending myself as best I could against the blows raining down over and over, I tried to grab the stick. It was when he crashed the weapon into my head that I lost what was left of the temper I was struggling to control. I pushed out at him and as he lost his balance I got a firm grip of the stick. He was still calling me for everything when the red mist descended. There was a blur as I laid into him with both fists, smashing his face into a bloody pulp. It all came out and the more he bled, the harder I hit. He was on the floor with me sitting on top of him, battering him for all I was worth until I was hauled away by my mum, who had heard the commotion. Breathless, I quickly dressed and ran into the park across from the house. I could have killed him. I could have killed my grandad. I'd been there before with my mother and vowed never to return. But I had, I had. It would be many years before I finally absorbed the maxim that those who choose not to remember the mistakes of the past are condemned to repeat them.

I sat on a bench in Holyrood Park, sobbing uncontrollably. I had done serious damage to one of the few people I knew loved me and had ever shown me kindness. Remarkably, my grandad allowed me to continue staying with him. He had been a violent man all his life and no doubt this wasn't the only time he had settled for the silver medal. But riddled with guilt and self-loathing, I resorted to self-harming again. The bloodshed had to be balanced and as soon as I had carved several stripes in my arms, in my fucked-up, disturbed way I considered justice had been done.

17

Caught

1987–88

'Hiya, Jeff, remember me?'

Those four words changed my life. They came from the smaller of two passing young women as I got off a bus. I recognised the larger girl but was clueless as to who the short, hazel-eyed lassie in the black clothes with the mad hair actually was. The tone in which she had spoken suggested we had been previously acquainted but my disdainful shake of the head accompanied by a curt 'Naw!' told her otherwise, as I turned my back on her and walked across the road and into the pub.

The two girls followed and before long I had paired off with the smaller one, Cath. I didn't really know her but she told me that she had been in the year below me at school and was adamant that we had at least spoken a few times. It didn't really matter. I had to admit that I did like her after a while and she made it obvious that she liked me, too.

We headed into town together and after having a few drinks in a Hanover Street pub, we found ourselves snogging inside a bus shelter. Neither of us could have had any idea of what lay in store for us. That night, I was flattered by the attention Cath lavished on me and excited by her disposition. We walked hand-in-hand towards our old school, where, in the middle of the night on a secluded bench, we almost, but not quite, had sex. I was pretty much out of my depth that night and it took all my powers of restraint to contain my excitement at being with this girl. We eventually parted at 7 a.m. after having a sobering coffee together in the railway station. I knew I would phone her sooner rather than later and as I lay back on my bed clutching the wee bit of paper with her number scrawled on it, I enjoyed the new sensation of being found attractive.

Within a week, we were having sex and within a month, we were spending every spare minute of our time together. That initial sexually charged period of discovery was one of the happiest times of my life. On the downside, I was too needy and within a few months I had convinced myself that I had found the 'one' at the first time of asking. I loved Cath and I wanted to spend the rest of my life with her. I couldn't imagine being without her, as things had started improving for me since she had become a part of my life.

Three weeks into our relationship, I got an office job in the Civil Service. Only a month before, I had felt worthless and hopeless; now I had a steady girlfriend, a proper job, some money and a stab at a future. All I needed to complete the set was to find somewhere to live on my own. It was time. Time to go and stand on my own two wobbly feet.

The trouble between Cath and I began almost immediately after I'd been allocated a council house in run-down Wester Hailes. This area of Edinburgh came as a complete culture shock. I invited Cath to move into a squalid one-bedroom ground-floor flat. Predictably, after a few weeks, we were in chaos.

We hadn't the first idea what we were doing and although the sex remained as regular and good as ever, the more fundamental parts of the relationship began to disintegrate. I'd lost my job by just not turning up, preferring to stay in bed with Cath. We were sleeping on two odd-sized single mattresses pushed together on the uncarpeted floor in the bedroom. We had no fridge or washing machine and what little furniture we did have was shabby oddments from friends. Looking around, I think I could have been forgiven for feeling strong déjà vu, as this was just how I had lived with my mum. If the truth were told, neither of us was equipped to cope with the desperate situation we had created for ourselves.

I don't actually remember the first time I hit Cath.

What I do know is that it wasn't the last.

Before we lived together, we'd never had a cross word. The flat was directly beneath a couple we became friendly with and we often heard them arguing and fighting. In the days afterwards, the woman would often be seen wearing a pair of dark glasses. At that time, very inexperienced in relationship matters, I was heavily influenced by this almost constant state of affairs. It seemed to me to be what couples who lived together did. It was the norm. Added to my inbuilt anger problem, this was a recipe for disaster.

Like my mother, Cath was plagued by PMT and would often act irrationally, which would in turn provoke me into fits of equally irrational violence. Perhaps it triggered memories of my mother's anger, perhaps not, but once the first blow was struck it was too late for analysis. I do recall Cath challenging me to hit her on one occasion when she was at her most volatile, and when I did, she challenged me again. It's no excuse but I was influenced by how we were living, by the lives of neighbours immersed in a cycle of domestic violence and by the way this behaviour seemed to be normalised.

I had started to break into cars and shops after I'd lost my job. I was doing this regularly, so the law of averages meant that it was only a matter of time before I got caught. On one late-night thieving expedition, a mate and I, without any reason, decided to try to steal a set of alloy wheels from a couple of cars we had seen earlier that day. Neither of us had a car that was compatible with the wheels: in fact, I was ten years away from passing my test, but it seemed like a good idea at the time. After a bit of a struggle with the jack, we eventually managed to swipe the wheels, load them into my mate's car and deliver them to my scabby wee flat. Some unseen curtain-twitching busybody with nothing else to do at two in the morning must have seen us and called the cops, who arrived the next morning to find the wheels in my cupboard.

This, my first arrest and subsequent charge, would result in my second criminal conviction. I was yet to commit the crime that would have the dubious honour of being my first, and it would be Cath that was my first victim.

Cath had a thing for randomly moving around what furniture we had in the sitting room. I had come in on a wet Saturday afternoon while Cath was doing some ironing in the sitting room and sat down on what I thought was the settee. Pre-occupied with drying off, I hadn't noticed that she had shifted everything around yet again and as I fell flat on my arse, banging my head off the wall where the sofa used to be, I lost it big time. I fucking hated all her mini-flittings – could she not just fucking leave things where they were? I hated her obsession with her hair – the fucking incessant racket of her fucking hairdryer and the constant cloying sting of her cheap solidifying hairspray. I hated everything about her at that moment in time.

All my pedantic pet-hates came out in a breathless volley of obscenities. It wasn't until she threw the still-hot iron at me that I punched her until her lips bled and her eye sockets turned into puffballs.

It was true.

I was shit.

When it was all over, I knew that I had hurt Cath more than ever and that this time sorry wouldn't do it. Without saying a word, she put on her coat and left.

It didn't take me long to realise that I wanted her back. I was alone and abandoned with nobody else to blame, plainly unable to cope in my shitty flat. I was crumbling. I dwelt upon the good times we'd shared, conveniently allowing the rest to fade.

After a week or so, I convinced myself that I could repair the damage. I walked to where Cath was living at her mum's house. As I walked, I became more and more certain that I could persuade her to return and felt confident that we could sort things out if she would just talk to me.

As I got closer to the house, I saw Cath sitting in the sun, her bruised and swollen face partially hidden behind big black sunglasses. Apart from the obvious damage to her face, Cath appeared fresh and clean, wearing brightly coloured, well-laundered clothes, and evidently relaxed. In the time she had been gone, she had been transformed, while I remained a shambolic mess. At that moment, I realised that I really was to blame for everything, as I saw then it had been me that had dragged Cath down to sewer level. She was getting on far better without me in her life. Still, I could try. I attracted Cath's attention and she came out onto the pavement where I stood, basically to tell me to fuck off. Things went red again and boiling anger flowed as I attacked her, the habit seemingly unbreakable, first with a ferocious butt to her head and then with my fists. I had done it again but this time the guilt and sorrow I felt had to be purged immediately.

I was a disgrace and after a few minutes running around, frantic with panic, I presented myself at the nearest police station, admitting through a series of unrestrained sobs that I had committed an as yet unreported crime. I was upset and emotional, which made it difficult for the officer to make any sense of my confession. It took four hours to complete the procedure during which I was photographed and fingerprinted and my confession was corroborated, resulting in my being charged with assault. I was released on bail and told to expect a summons to appear at court.

The torment began to eat away at me slowly, starting that night, until it would take me to a point where I would, a few weeks later, take a massive overdose of drugs from the medicine cabinet in my mother's friend's bathroom. It was my court appearance for the assault that would be the catalyst that took me deeper into the abyss.

In June 1988, Edinburgh Sheriff Court was situated on the corner of the High Street and the Mound. I sat on the public benches, alone, waiting for the clerk to call my name. I had only ever seen a courtroom on TV and was clueless as to any of the procedures. I expected to go into the dock, say I was guilty and take whatever punishment the judge deemed appropriate. As I sat shaking in my cheap, grey, iron-shined suit and scuffed black shoes, the terrifying thought of prison was never far away.

Finally, I heard my name being shouted and made my way into the dock. After the Procurator Fiscal had outlined the specifics of my case, silence descended as all eyes turned towards me. I pled guilty and was given a £150 fine and £350 compensation order (to be paid at £5 a week). I went back to the flat in Wester Hailes. There was no way that I could have contacted Cath, as I would no doubt have been arrested and probably jailed. None of my family knew what was going on at that time, so I was, in every sense, alone.

I deserved it.

18

Try Again

10 July 1988

I am in a bathroom that is not familiar to me. I look at the face reflected in the cabinet and that, too, is no longer familiar to me. I reach out and replace the view with one of small shelves on which sit boxes and bottles, packets and jars, all containing things that I know can take me to the place I want to go. The words on the containers mean nothing to me but they look impressive. They all end in 'ine' and 'ol'.

I empty the contents of them all into my hands and as I run the cold tap beneath the cabinet I am fascinated by the colours of the mixture of drugs that sit harmlessly in the palm of my hand: there are yellow ones, slightly bigger than the rest, in the shape of rugby balls; there are wafer-thin pink ones and a varied selection of white ones of differing shapes; there are translucent green gel-filled capsules glinting at me from underneath a small cluster of blue and black plastic-coated capsules in the shape of small bullets. Highly appropriate, I think to myself. I will fire these into my brain and I will be no more.

This lethal cocktail is my passport to a better place and I am ready to travel.

I don't think any more.

I drink.

89

I drink the cold water and ready my throat to swallow the multicoloured array of bullets. I feel nothing. I have a purpose and I will follow it through to the end.

I'm not scared. Pain is what I'm escaping from. I am running away from feeling alone. If I am to be alone, then I will be alone on my terms. I won't be abandoned again. I will not allow myself to be rejected again. Soon there will be nothing left to reject and I will have my revenge. I will make them sorry.

I feel as if I am falling fast into a bright light that gets brighter as it slowly sucks the last of the light left in me. There is no pain, only disorientation. The cable has snapped and I feel myself plummet, my internal organs rising as they struggle against the rush of the pills. I'm comforted by the external light and try to move my body closer towards its source. As I stand (for it feels as though I am still standing, although I am at right angles to everything else), semi-conscious, in these barely recognisable and increasingly blurred and surreal surroundings, the last thing I see is the face of the madness hovering above me.

I have fallen.

The darkness is my friend and I won't relinquish it without a fight; there is more light burning my eyes and then a coldness vomiting from my most internal parts. I feel a blow to my body, and then another, and another still. More cold, more blows, but thankfully no more light. The blows recede and the cold is no more. I am floating, suspended between the light and the dark. And then nothing.

Nothing at all.

I am roused by a soft feminine whisper. 'Wake up. Wake up.' Over and over.

'Wake up!'

I am not dead.

I did not die.

I have lost several days of my life in the build-up to my suicide attempt and in the time I have spent recovering in hospital. For that small consolation, I'm grateful. As my senses return, I see that I'm in a strange bed in a vast room with many similar strange beds. The whisper belongs to a woman dressed in bright white. She says I must go. She says that the duty psychiatrist who has assessed me in a five-minute slot believes I am fit for discharge. She hands me a clipboard and a pen that I use to sign the discharge form and as she walks away I find my clothes and dress myself.

Now I'm walking. Walking aimlessly from the building where my body has been lying, reluctantly alive. I have no idea whether anyone knows what has happened, whether anyone has visited me, whether anyone cares.

I'm alive and I'm alone, drifting along, alone in the crowd, hoping to find a way out.

Again, again, again.

19

The Real Deal

1988–89

It took me almost as many months as the relationship had lasted to, at least superficially, get over Cath, and that was only because I threw myself head first straight into another one. I made no attempt to contact Cath after either my court appearance or my suicide attempt, and that was a relatively sensible thing for me to do.

With a serious suicide attempt not far behind me, and a habit of self-harm, I'd been attending twice-weekly counselling sessions at a voluntary mental-health group. Ostensibly, my life improved in the six months after my first court appearance, even when I was handed a £60 fine for the theft of the wheels a couple of months later. I had found a half-decent job with a firm of sheriff officers, which, with overtime, paid well and introduced me to a lot of normal, decent people.

The only real downside was that I'd returned to live with my mum. I'd lasted less than a year in Wester Hailes: unable to cope on my own, I had left a mountain of unopened bills and a flat in squalor. The very last time I had been in the flat in the autumn of 1988, the bathroom was disgusting: rodent carcasses crawling with plump maggots in the bath and bluebottles buzzing around everywhere. The electricity had long since been disconnected and so, on seeing this mess, I did what I always did in a crisis: I ran and never looked back.

The house in St Leonard's was still a shambles and my mum and I still grated on each other, so I drifted back up the stair to my grandad and took up residence in 'the room'. This time was different. I was a working man and my grandad was brilliant, waking me in the mornings with breakfast, making sure I left in time for work. We talked about everything and it was only at this late stage in his life that I began to see him not just as my grandad but as a man who had lived a hell of a life himself.

Not long after starting my new job in the late summer of 1988, a woman I had never seen around the office before was standing in front of me at the coffee vending machine. A vision in blonde with deeply tanned skin and piercing ice-blue eyes, she was stunning, but I knew my place. Look but don't even think about hoping to touch. She was miles out of my league and so the thought of anything happening between us, the goddess and the fat fuck-up, was preposterous.

After that first sighting of Leanne, there was very little contact between us. Working together obviously meant we would sometimes pass the time of day but on my part I assumed that was as far as it could ever go.

The night after what was to be my last appointment at the mental-health group was also the office Christmas party. I had taken a wager with my boss to see which one of us would wear the most ostentatious outfit. Wearing a hired white tuxedo, wide-brimmed hat and green bow tie, I won easily. I'd decided that I was going along just for a giggle, so it was to my delight that the seating arrangements placed me next to Leanne. We chatted a lot and when the lights went down for the disco, she even got me up dancing – no mean feat. My inhibitions were evaporating slowly but, never really the quickest on the uptake, I was oblivious to her advances, although as the night went on the alcohol certainly started to loosen me up. The consequences of making a move stopped being such an issue.

After the party ended with a slow dance with Leanne, a coachload of us were taken up town to a nightclub. She slid her hand into mine as easily as she had chatted to me all night and once inside we stood in a space near the end of the bar, snogging away without a thought for what any of our workmates might say. Without breaking away from each other, we made our way to the corner that had been reserved for our party and carried on where we had left off.

I felt as if a magic spell had removed all the crap from my life there and then. Leanne had a very powerful effect on me, which only intensified when we went on to someone's flat with two other couples. As I sat on the floor with her cuddled into my side, I thought I'd gone to Heaven. Before she left with one of the other girls, she wrote down her number and whispered for me to call her soon.

I called her the next evening from a phone box. I was nervous but had the courage to ask her out the following night and I was more delighted than I let on when she said yes.

I approached life that winter with an uncharacteristic spring in my step but deep inside my demons were only hibernating in order to regain their strength and attack when I would least expect it in what would be, so far, their finest hour.

On the night of 1 January 1989, three weeks after first getting together, we sat alone in Leanne's parents' house, where she still lived, before going on to a New Year party. It was consummation time. Leanne was the real deal. I was awestruck. We walked to the party with me unable to wipe the gormless grin from my face and it was fairly obvious to the folk at our pal's house that we had taken things to the next level.

While we were together, Leanne never allowed her relationships with her many pals to be compromised. On occasion, I would socialise with them as well but generally I had my time with her and they had theirs. With these limits in place, it meant that I really looked forward to seeing her. After going out together for six weeks or so, we were sitting on a park bench, chatting away. I always kept my past, particularly the many dark areas, concealed by jokes. That night Leanne innocently remarked that we'd yet to have a serious conversation and surely I had another side to me. With that innocuous comment she had opened the door to the real me – only slightly but for the things I had to reveal, only slightly was far too much. That was it – she simply said to me, in Inverleith Park

94

on a cold Wednesday night, 'We've been going out for six weeks and never had a serious conversation.'

Nothing more.

But it was enough, enough to shake the demons and give them the chance they wanted to get prepared for battle.

One of the more positive things that developed as my relationship with Leanne continued was my previously unknown romantic side. I'd buy flowers, champagne, silly wee toys, write poems or letters, or perhaps organise surprise trips or evenings out, always with a personal touch — something like a celebration of a specific time or date. Leanne inspired me to all sorts of romantic gestures and it was during my time with her that I discovered that I was, in every sense, far happier giving than receiving. To this day, I'm uncomfortable when given things, particularly from a partner. I get a much bigger thrill when I am giving ostentatious presents or spending extravagantly on others, which no doubt has its roots in my early years when I felt materially deprived. I was also, albeit with the most altruistic of intentions, simply buying love and attention because I felt unworthy of receiving these things just for being myself. I was confusing money with love as well as sex. However, at 20, while as insecure as I was always going to be, I did not have the self-perception to realise the dangerous habit I had started or where it could, and ultimately would, lead me. That lesson would be 16 years in the learning.

Although I'd spent some time with Leanne at the home she shared with her parents, it was a while before I actually met them properly, as whenever I was round at the house they would be on their way to, or already down at, the local bowling club. This gave us the opportunity to have a few glasses of wine and obligatory sex. On the last Saturday of every month, the bowling club organised a social night where members could invite a few guests to share in the weekend festivities. At the end of January 1989, I attended the soirée to be unveiled as Leanne's 'official' new bloke. I was really nervous, not only about meeting her parents but also about having to socialise with people I had never met before. In less than half an hour, I had tanned a litre bottle of wine in the sitting room and while on the surface I remained calm and gregarious, even when we took the short walk round the corner to the club, I was shitting myself.

After being introduced properly to Leanne's mum and dad and the rest of the company, I attacked the drink with gusto. Before too long, with more down me, I had completely relaxed. I actually got confident enough to extrovertly hold court and have them roaring with laughter. Things were going swimmingly well when I was politely informed it was my turn to get a round in. Off I went to the bar, accompanied by Leanne's dad, who, with the round consisting of around 20 separate drinks for the 13 or so in it, knew I would need a hand carrying them back. While waiting for the drinks, Leanne's dad got me involved in a frenzy – downing as much as I could as quickly as I could. In the time it took for the round to be ready, we had shared the cost of eight Bacardi and cokes. That was four healthy measures of spirits in less than five minutes and it wasn't even nine o'clock.

Everybody in the company bought at least two rounds. Even while I felt not too drunk, it was apparent that with the contents of a big bottle of wine, four Bacardis, in excess of sixteen pints and about ten vodkas, I was well on my way to being in a wee bit of bother. I'd never drunk so much in such a short space of time but it had seemed impolite to refuse. I didn't notice just how bad I was until I turned to talk to the woman who was sat next to me, Leanne's mum's best pal. I knew what I wanted to say, I even knew how I was going to say it, but when my mouth finally engaged with what was left of my pickled brain, all I remember is drunkenly announcing to the world that I was 'gauntaerrrlavvyfurapish' ('I intend to transport myself to the nearest available lavatory in order that I relieve the overwhelmingly uncomfortable pressing sensation I am currently experiencing in my bladder, which my brain has interpreted as an urgent requirement to urinate'), before removing my now elasticated body from my seat and falling, face first, smack-bang on the edge of the dance floor.

I'm not sure if I did find the ability to urinate but what a splendid impression I must have made in the company of my new girlfriend's parents.

When I awoke the next morning in Leanne's bedroom, the first thing that registered was the familiar acrid taste of vomit in my nose and throat. My mouth was a bit dry but the only real suggestion of a hangover was that overwhelming feeling of guilt without really knowing what it is that you feel guilty about.

As I slowly got my head together, ensuring that I didn't make any sudden movements in case my hangover was lulling me into a false sense of security, I realised I was naked. I saw that my clothes had been folded into a neat pile on the other side of the room, which only fuelled my embarrassment even more as obviously someone had undressed me and put me to bed. And as if that wasn't bad enough, I could now hear movement coming from somewhere else in the house. With a swift escape out of the question, I got up, hurriedly dressed and gingerly crept through to the living room to face whatever music awaited me.

'You were in some state last night, were ye no?' Leanne's dad said from behind his newspaper, which was just far enough below his face for me to see him smirking benevolently.

'Aye, I know. Sorry,' I replied, fascinated all of a sudden by the weave of the carpet underneath my bare feet. 'I didn't mean to cause any trouble.'

'Don't worry, you were fine,' a female voice said just loud enough for me to hear from the adjoining kitchen, from where the sounds and smells of a Sunday fry-up were wafting through. 'C'mon through and get your breakfast,' Leanne's mum said. Without actually realising it, I was really hungry, not having eaten for at least 24 hours. My performance of the previous night was laughed off and, although I'd apparently been carried up the road by Leanne and her mum, nobody seemed to mind. From that weekend on, I would spend more or less every Saturday night and well into Sunday evening at Leanne's, sometimes even getting up first and taking the dog for a walk. It became a good habit as we got into a comfortable routine, with things like doing the newspaper crossword becoming almost traditional. What could have been a disastrous first proper meeting with my girlfriend's parents turned out really well. They had accepted me immediately and I really took to them, particularly her mother, who was a warm, wise, kind lady. To this day, I deeply regret what happened at the end of my relationship with Leanne, not only because of the pain I caused her but also because a mother always feels the pain of her child. I wish I could undo what happened – not for my sake, as that was my destiny and would have happened regardless, but for Leanne and her family, who did not know, could not know, what I'd bring to their lives.

Leanne soon changed jobs and so our Wednesdays and Saturdays were even more special, as I didn't see her at work during the day any more. Even after going out for six months or so, whenever we met in town I would still look at her and have to pinch myself, as I thought I was the jammiest bastard in the world. But one of the biggest problems with going out with one of the beautiful people, especially for people like me with an abundance of emotional insecurities, is the trust issue. For absolutely no reason at all, I began to feel jealous when I knew Leanne was out with her friends. I didn't show this, and I don't have any reason to believe that Leanne knew of it, but, nonetheless, it was how I felt.

One night in the summer of 1989, Leanne told me, when she arrived back, that she'd kissed someone else on holiday. I had challenged her after one of her friends had inadvertently dropped her in it by saying, 'Leanne would never go behind your back.' The comment was completely out of the blue but it set me thinking. Why was there an unprovoked denial of something that had never been raised? Was something being hidden behind it? I raised it with Leanne and she was genuinely apologetic – she was 22, on holiday with mates and I was about to blow it up out of all proportion. I felt hurt, cheated, jealous – I'd been right not to trust her all along, I thought. It was nothing more than a drunken snog in a Mediterranean nightclub but I was just unable to deal with the thought of it emotionally.

By day, I just about managed to keep the most tenuous of grips on my public face with people who were unimportant to me, the people we all have to interact with but have no emotional investment in. By night, when alone, my fantasies about committing bizarre forms of self-harm would go very close to breaking what barriers were still containing me. I was dangerously closing in on the edge of my private, painful abyss. The fantasy was on the verge of becoming a hellish, ugly reality.

20

Goodbyes

1989–90

One Wednesday night after I had engineered a trivial argument with Leanne, who was by this time becoming more and more bewildered about what was happening to me, I put one of the most bloody of my night-time terrors into practice. I eased myself back into the mindset of my mid-teens and took a clean safety razor from a new pack of five I had purchased earlier that day. As before, I wrapped a piece of protective cotton round one end and while carefully and steadily holding a mirror in my right hand, I used my left to deeply etch a star-shaped scar into my left cheek – the star being a throwback to my childish vandalism many years before. The intricate cutting took a few minutes to complete and this time I was concentrating so hard I felt no pain at all, only a sense of supreme triumph and comfort that intensified as I watched the reflection of my face soaking with fresh blood as it seeped from the grotesque mark that I carved into my flesh. I felt satisfied as I stood in the bathroom, the silence broken only by the sounds of my regular breathing and the splashing of the viscous liquid as it fell from my chin, rapidly tip-tapping a solo beat into the dark-red pool forming around my feet. Feeling and seeing the blood empty from this new wound filled me with a sense of vindication. For what, however, I do not know. All I knew was that the metronomic sensation of the warm, sticky fluid pulsating from this new rip in my flesh felt good, and I stood and enjoyed it for as long as I possibly could. I knew also that I would have to go to hospital to be patched up as, due to the unusual shape I had made on my face, it would not heal naturally and in any case I had sliced virtually all the way through to the inside of my mouth.

At the hospital, I came up with an elaborate lie to explain the odd injury, something about being jumped by a guy with blades melted into a lead knuckleduster. The hospital informed the police and I ended up creating a whole dramatic episode for them, even going as far as identifying someone from their collection of 'mug shots' as bearing a bit of a resemblance to my 'attacker'. Thankfully the police investigation went nowhere but in my calmer moments I knew that I had gone too far. I was, as usual in the wake of these monstrous assaults on myself, ashamed and embarrassed, but I had to follow the whole charade through and so I repeated the story with increasing embellishment to anyone who asked about the star-shaped cut on my face. I have only ever admitted the truth about this incident to Leanne and one other person, who knows who they are. To those I deceived and who believed my lie – I am sorry.

My 21st birthday came and went without ceremony. In March, disillusioned, I resigned from my job with the sheriff officers. By that time, I was taking home a decent wage supplemented by abuse of the overtime schedule, which was one of my responsibilities. At the end of every month, in those pre-computerised days, I collected all the overtime sheets and had them authorised and signed by the boss before dispatching them to the wages department in a separate building. I always worked at least one hour of overtime each month so that I had a form to fill in and when my sheet had been signed and authorised I added anything from 35 to 70 extra hours – a good few extra quid in my bank account the next week for a couple of minutes' creativity with a blue biro. Nobody ever questioned my wages and often I was being paid for six weeks' work in every four. But even that and a few other minor fiddles involving manual payments and the petty cash weren't enough to keep me working there, so off I went, back into the world of supplementary benefit and long days in front of the telly waiting for the giro to drop through the letter box. Leanne was noncommittal about all of this – it was obvious that I was in trouble, that I was sinking, but she clearly didn't want to dig too deeply.

My grandad had died by this time and it had hit me harder than I ever thought it would. We had grown closer over the years and I had enjoyed his company as a man. I could listen to him for hours as he reflected on his life. I felt frustrated anger and deep regret, because I had never told him at any time in my life that, regardless of the many ups and downs we had had, I loved him dearly. While on the surface I appeared to cope with the things that were happening to me, my grandad's death had further compromised my rapidly fragmenting sanity. By then I was living in a bedsit in a run-down area and the edges of my depression really began to lacerate me. On one occasion, I recall Leanne coming into my room as I sat in the corner, rocking back and forth whilst weeping my breaking heart out. She was visibly shocked and seemed at a loss as to how to react. The relationship I had with Leanne was a means of escape from the despair I felt. I invested far too much in what we had, or didn't have, together – as I had always done. I was losing it big time and I descended into an absolute mess over the next few months.

In the summer, I sat on the edge of my single bed in my grotty room and made a very deep perpendicular cut high up on the inside of my left wrist with a razor blade. As the blood wept from this gaping slit, I kept wiping it clean until I had cut deep enough to see the thin membrane enclosing the pulsating artery. With a morbid fascination, I fought my fear. It was the first time that I truly contemplated my own death. I have never been frightened of death – that is, actually being dead – but the process of dying, the body gradually shutting down, terrifies me.

At the time I slashed my wrist, I was desperate to confront my own death but I bottled out and went to hospital to be stitched. As opposed to the fabulous lies that had accompanied my previous acts of cutting, on this occasion there was nothing ambiguous about my wound.

I knew that I had problems, and had been spending many evenings trawling telephone directories to find the numbers of relevant agencies who could perhaps offer help. Until this point, no one from within the medical profession had actually questioned what was going on; they seemed perfectly content to accept my explanations and, as far as I know, I was certainly never recorded or labelled as a suicide risk. My medical records bear this out.

It was obvious, however, that I did need help and this was as loud a plea for it as I would ever make. I was advised impatiently and disdainfully that I should seek urgent psychiatric assistance as soon as I possibly could and for once I did what I was told.

Two days later, with my wrist heavily bandaged, Leanne accompanied me to the Royal Edinburgh Hospital to see the emergency duty psychiatrist. It was obvious that I was in trouble but I clammed up, letting Leanne do most of the talking. The doctor gave me some reassuring words of wisdom and I was basically told that only time would heal me and I would be all right in the end. In retrospect, given what happened afterwards, this may sound like neglect on the part of the hospital but they were unable to assess me properly and realise just what was happening to me. I was self-deprecating, apologetic and inarticulate when I did speak for myself. I focused more on trying to impress the doctor with my masquerade rather than tell the truth about how things were. The details of the sexual assault were locked away in a place where even I couldn't reach them, so it was hardly surprising that I was deemed to be no more than a wee bit upset. Very few people actually witnessed the extent to which I had sunk. That year had so many endings for me – the end of my job and my grandad's life, my relationship with Leanne was coming to a close and even (if I had known it) the end of my life without a crippled body. I was still hanging on to my mask of 'normality' by the thinnest of threads. There was one man left in the world who I believed could strengthen that thread but in the event he was the one man I should have known would, in reality, wield the scissors that would cut me off from it completely.

My dad.

102

21

That's What Dads Do...

1990

When Leanne went off on holiday in August, things were pretty close to breaking point between us. I had become far too needy and difficult for the girl who just wanted to have a good time. Getting away from me and my nonsense must have been a huge relief for her – a time to consider the decision she knew she had to make, and rightly so.

In her absence, chewed up with jealousy and insecurity, I made the huge mistake of succumbing to my need for love from my father. I knew in my heart that he really didn't want to know but I needed him more than I ever had. I wanted my dad to fix everything for me – that's what dads do, isn't it?

Not mine.

I should have known better but as I sat on the overnight bus to London, then on to the town where he lived, I was hoping against hope that he might be able to offer me some kind of help. I didn't know what to expect when I got to his house but the sight of an obese, ginger-haired woman sitting at home on the sofa in the small living room threw me even further off-guard. She would have been my second stepmother.

I made out to my father that I was 'just passing' but my nervousness and rapid-fire edgy talking should have indicated that all was far from right with me. I wanted to scream at Ray, to beg him to act, for once, like my dad – but it didn't feel natural. He had let me down. Again.

I arrived at his home on the Wednesday afternoon. He said so little to me that it would be ridiculous to even suggest there were conversations between us. On the Friday morning, he drove me into the centre of town, from where I caught a bus back to Edinburgh. He said nothing of significance. The man was reluctant to conduct a conversation of any sort, even though it was transparently obvious that I, his son, was a mess.

I was worth nothing, not even the natural love of a father for his son. I was crushed. It was now only a matter of time before this latest in the catalogue of rejection would be compounded, taking me ever closer, ever faster, to what was my destiny. I recall very little of the journey back to Edinburgh other than a resigned feeling of inadequacy.

The night before the day that was to change my life, I sat alone on a rock in the middle of a litter-strewn field, staring blankly across the Firth of Forth. I knew that something truly awful was on the verge of happening but at that moment I didn't know what. I had no plans. I reflected on the loneliness I had felt when a child: the emptiness that had increased as experience had filled my life with more emptiness. I couldn't pinpoint the root of my problems. I puzzled over why I'd never felt as if I'd belonged anywhere, always destined to be the spectator, the outsider. I saw myself as fat, ugly and unattractive in every way. Even though I had a beautiful girlfriend, I knew it was only a matter of hours before it was confirmed that I would be, once again, unattached. Detached. Disconnected. I had pushed her away.

I analysed my inability to love and accept love the way normal people could. I picked away at the scabs of myself, mulling over the details of the violence I had suffered and inflicted upon others. I had not considered myself to be a violent person but as I dug and dug, deeper and deeper, I saw that violence of the rawest sort had come to underline the story of my life. I had been surrounded by it all my life.

Terrified and out of my mind with despair, it was almost time – and I felt so fucking lonely. I was alone with my destiny. A destiny that I had no control over but to which I would peacefully surrender if it promised to take the pain away. I would deliver myself to a better place, where the torment couldn't follow and where my soul could escape its perpetual torturers. I knew, somehow, it was time. Time to go. I was ready.

I stood up from the rock and broke into a natural run, back to where I lived. Amongst all the psychological debris that I was fighting to make sense of, the one thing that I gave not a single thought to was the fact that I was running. Running flat out and taking it for granted. It was all I was left still able to do. I ran and ran and ran. Until I could run no more. I loved to run and had done so all my life. Always running. Running away, but running all the same. Never giving it a second thought. Why is it, I wonder now, that the things we value the most are the things that we pay the least attention to? Until, of course, we no longer have them.

I didn't sleep that night. I sat on the floor for hours with nothing in my head except the knowledge that the next day was Sunday – the day Leanne had said she was coming to visit after returning from her holiday. Maybe she had missed me when she was on holiday and would declare undying love for me. Maybe she would have the answers she knew I was so desperately searching for.

Maybe not.

As the day lumbered on, I became more and more anxious and insecure. I had invested, yet again, far too much in Leanne. The more I needed for myself, the more of myself I had given away. It had come to this. I was at the bottom of the barrel, with no money, few possessions, no hope, no friends (I'd turned my back on them) and no future. My self-esteem was as non-existent as my self-respect and there I was, waiting for the only person who had stuck by me so far.

Hanging out of the top-flat window, checking the street below (again), I saw the elegant figure of a tall, blonde, golden-brown female turning into the street in the distance and, as always when I saw Leanne, my heart skipped a few beats. In my head, I re-rehearsed what I'd say after I had given her the planned hug. I'd put on an act of happiness and pretend I had sorted myself out and assure her that things would get better. I'd tell her how great she looked and that I had really missed her (which I had). I would apologise profusely for all the heartache I had caused and swear that the future was bright. I would try not to appear too needy while keeping things nice and light and once again play the part of the guy who 'made her laugh all the time'. As the Sunday-night radio chart show played on, the doorbell heralded the arrival of my new beginning. Soon, I thought, I would be lying on my back staring dreamily upward at the most beautiful girl in the world. As I followed Leanne into my room, this was to be the last throw of the dice in the crap game that was my life. Despite my determination to appear calm and normal, inside I felt hysterical. But if the rejection had not occurred, it would have been an excuse not to jump at the time – or, in reality, to postpone jumping.

The look of steely determination in Leanne's eyes as she stood, refusing to sit, in the centre of my room set the tone without a word being uttered. It was over. She didn't have to say it. I knew. It was the last of my fears to be realised and the demons unleashed themselves with an unprecedented fury. Almost at once, every single wound I had suffered burst open, spewing pure self-loathing. I was haemorrhaging raw hatred from every delicate emotional scar. At once I was free but I was trapped. Not yet dead but no longer alive. I had been animalised. Animalised by my life, by myself and by my past. My destiny was not in my hands; it was in the hands of the madness. Nothing mattered except fulfilling my destiny.

I leapt onto the window ledge and stood, looking down, not worried about the distance being too great but too little. I wasn't scared. Hyperventilating, I prepared myself to jump but as I did so Leanne somehow convinced me to get down. Very quickly, however, the tension between us elevated to raised voices until, delirious with frustrated, defeated anguish, my head virtually exploded with the sheer violence of what was happening to me.

My anxiety reached its deafening crescendo. I defiantly, deliberately and yet almost dispassionately ran the few steps back towards the wide open top-flat window and, without touching the sides or the sill, leapt into the nothingness beyond, emitting a low, beastly, guttural growl as I did so. It would be over soon and I was glad. I was falling away from whatever had kept me from falling for far too long. It was my only means of escape, the only way to be delivered from evil. The evil that had brought me to be falling – falling to the gutter where I believed I belonged.

22

The Boy Becomes a Man

AUGUST–NOVEMBER 1990

At the moment of impact, I didn't feel a thing. Everything just came to an abrupt stop.

My body had taken a severe blow but my mind took a few minutes to catch up. I was lying, contorted, face down on the concrete-clad ground and yet, physically, I felt not too bad – a wee bit numb around the ankles but nothing worse than a heavy tackle from a bruising centre-forward. I thought I could probably get up and walk it off. Before I tried to get on my feet, I twisted my neck in order to inspect what, if any, damage I had done to my legs. As I did so, my eyes caught a glimpse of a blonde head darting back from the window I had leapt from only seconds before: the blonde head that had provided the catalyst for this failed act of self-destruction. The blonde head that I had convinced myself I loved.

Leanne. Fuck! What had I just done? Not to me but to her. Her rejection of me gave me the final push that I needed. I needed something to blame at that precise moment and she gave me it. I made her watch. She didn't deserve that. My life was mine and mine alone to end. My body was mine to destroy. I had no business involving anybody else. I should have known better than to paint her a gruesome picture that she would no doubt remember for the rest of her life. I didn't care at the

107

time, the time of jumping or preparing to jump. It was to be my final statement and she was to be my witness. It is often said that suicide is a selfish act. Of course it is. That's the whole point. When a mind is tortured enough to want to wipe itself out for ever, how can anyone or anything else matter? When I saw Leanne from the ground, in a moment of clarity, ridiculous as it may appear, I did think of what I had done to her. My mind was racing with emotions – not least of which was guilt.

I wasn't prepared for the sight that faced me as my gaze settled on my legs. One of my shinbones had shot through the back of my calf. There was at least six inches of bone protruding from an angry red aperture. I felt what blood I had left in my face, which felt strangely cold and clammy, drain away. And it was then that the pain hit. I'd felt physical pain before but this was from another dimension. I saw bright silver sparks in my peripheral vision as I tried to focus on Leanne as she whispered comforting words to me. She informed me that an ambulance was on its way. 'Everything will be OK,' she soothed. We would go to Paris together, she said, when I got sorted out. I knew she was just saying what she thought I needed to hear. I know she meant well and no doubt was in shock herself but I knew. She couldn't look me in the eyes. She never would again.

I lay still, not daring to move. I felt every minute movement. The minutes felt like days. I was almost delirious with the pain, even though they quickly fed me gas through a plastic mask. All the while there were voices talking to me in hushed tones. 'OK, Jeff, on the count of three, we're going to lift you into the ambulance. Ready? One . . . two . . . three.' Right at that instant, I heard a scream. The worst noise I had ever heard. It took me a few seconds to realise it was coming from me. Never before or since has a sound of such pure, raw agony come from my body.

In the ambulance, Leanne sat with me, tenderly stroking my left hand as my eyes drifted. The siren screams drowned out my own. I had failed, succeeding only in crippling my body. A perfect partner for my crippled mind. Those were the terms that would define me from that moment on.

I was rushed straight through to the Royal Infirmary's A&E

department. By this time, I couldn't speak, only screech and wail. I could hear words and phrases that meant very little to me at the time, words such as 'amputation', 'never walk again' and, the most ironic of all, 'lucky to be alive'. I lost consciousness within a few minutes of my arrival at hospital and when I woke I had entered a new world. One to which, in time, I would adapt well, a system that seemed almost custom-designed for my needs. A system that afforded me 24-hour care and attention.

I came round in one of the trauma wards. I was very disorientated, emotionally and physically crushed. Most of all, though, I was hostile. Very, very hostile. There were tubes in my arms, nose and mouth. I was hooked up to machines via wires on my chest, stomach and shoulders. I was scared. My legs throbbed viciously and appeared to be encased in elevated rubber pillows. I could raise my head and look down but all that was visible were swollen toes. Nurses were fussing and around my bed were my mother, auntie, sister and various others, whose presence only just registered. I heard talk of operations, emergency operations. I was due to go to theatre, had I had anything to eat? Failing to understand the obvious significance of these questions, I began to get belligerent. While I was no stranger to hospitals, this was a whole new ball game. I wasn't there for some routine procedure that had been diligently planned and managed over a period of time; I was a failed suicide. A very painful, angry and cantankerous one at that.

I asked my mum how she knew I was in hospital and she told me Leanne had been in touch. She had waited in A&E until my mum turned up and then left the hospital. I've never seen her since. I hope her nightmares didn't last too long.

I had been given a painkilling injection but it was ineffective. I was distressed, barely coherent and begging anyone who would listen to please stop the pain. What happened next would have consequences that would reverberate for years. The impact of a simple act of kindness would be so monumental, not just on me but on those close to me, in the years ahead that, had I known, I would have refused to cooperate in order to prevent the pain it would cause to those I loved. If I had known, I would have chosen the physical agony I was experiencing at the time over the pain this benevolent act would cause later on.

The nurse took my wrist in her hand and asked me for my date of birth. I was puzzled. She knew my date of birth from my wristband. I started screaming at her, 'What the fuck do you want that for?', tears streaming down my cheeks. She told me she was going to take the pain away but first I had to tell her my date of birth. What the fuck was going on? I just wanted my pain gone, could she not see that? Even through the haze of my agony, I remained abusively stubborn until another nurse arrived at my bedside and explained the reasons for the date-of-birth questions – it was a rudimentary security approach to ensure that staff administered the correct drugs to the correct patient. Satisfied, I recited the appropriate numbers and was immediately plugged in to an intravenous infusion pump, filling my veins with a sweet clear liquid on a fast track to my brain.

Its magic worked instantaneously. My pain had gone. My lungs struggled for a moment to find air then quickly settled into a deep slow rhythm. I had been introduced to the delights of pharmaceutical-quality diamorphine hydrochloride . . . known to the wider world as heroin. I was on a very heavy dose and the drug made me feel like I could walk on water. I drifted in and out of sleep until I heard a metallic clatter. Suddenly the ceiling was moving. I tried to focus on the heavy-set, light-blue-clad man dragging my bed and contents out of its berth. I was being taken, for the first time, to the operating theatre, a journey that would become all too familiar over the next few weeks. My muddled mind briefly returned to that self-same floor I had trod 14 years ago when my granny died. Here I was again, surrounded by people yet alone with my fear. Surrounded by people I thought I should know, people who perhaps were close to me. People who did not matter to me, who behaved as if I hadn't mattered to them when I was a lonely, exposed, vulnerable seven-year-old boy shuffling through the corridors of this very building on the day my life changed for ever. I looked directly at my mum, who, alongside my auntie, had opted to accompany me to theatre. A stupid, childlike grin crept over my face and I sat straight up, punched the air and screamed madly in my mother's face, 'This is the fuuuckiin' business!' Even in my stupor, I was offering an act of defiance to my mum. I knew she hated the 'f' word and I knew that at that moment I could use it with impunity.

After the initial shock of hospital protocol and routine, I quickly settled into life on Ward 2. Patients came and went twenty-four hours a day, seven days a week. The heat on the ward was unbearable, particularly for those of us confined to lying on the plastic-wrapped mattresses. On one very warm day, I had my bed linen changed at least eight times to make sure I spent as little time as possible lying in a pool of my own sweat. No mean feat for the nursing staff, as it took at least six of them to change my bed. In the main, sleep patterns revolved around the timing of the drug trolley; time itself was meaningless to patients. I was still on the infusion pump, so the drugs round didn't affect me. With the physical trauma and the introduction of opiates into my system, my body underwent a series of rapid changes. In the fortnight I was on a constant supply of diamorphine, my weight plummeted from 13½ stone to less than 11 stone.

During the first few days, I felt I was being judged because of my apparent mental illness. I thought that all the staff, while being nice to me, considered me a nutcase behind my back. To combat this, I chattered away to any staff member who would listen to my story, trying to qualify what I had done to myself. Overwhelmed with guilt and the ever-present feelings of self-loathing, I would launch into a diatribe of justification. I would come up with all sorts of reasons to stop them from thinking I was a loony. I would talk about it being a moment of temporary madness, a reaction to events as opposed to something deeper-rooted.

Even after all that had happened, I was able to turn on the charm in an attempt to save face. Deep down, I was simply ashamed that I'd put so many people to so much trouble. As far as anyone else was concerned, it was agreed (for the sake of my mother's reputation, as much as anything else) that I had had an accident whilst cleaning windows. By that time I was already a very accomplished liar, with a lifetime of practice, and so I had no trouble convincing people that my injuries had been sustained accidentally: a lie I was able to maintain in public for a long time afterwards.

As a parent myself now, I can imagine that my mother must have been deeply upset – to outlive your child is an unimaginable horror and that is what she had faced. She knew that I had made suicide attempts in the past, but now I was a buckled, drugged-up mess with blood pissing out of my lower body, so an investigative dialogue between us wasn't really on the list of priorities at the time. Of course she visited me, and of course she asked how I was, but neither of us wanted to, or could, talk about what was really going on under the surface.

I was visited by psychiatrists, psychologists and social workers, and I found it easy enough to deflect their professional attention. I had no intention of revisiting my life for what I saw as the titillation of others; at least, that's how I justified it to myself. If the truth be told, I was vaguely aware of the demons that lay within me and I was in no way able to release and confront them. When speaking with these analysts, I would offer them no more than the fact that I had an argument with my girlfriend and a subsequent rush of blood that resulted in me jumping from the window. They never pressed me and seemed satisfied with my explanation. I just didn't cotton on to the fact that they had access to my medical history, which was littered with obvious examples of self-harm: incidents that, throughout the years, had painted a picture of a disturbed adolescent, incidents that, although accompanied with plausible background stories, were far too numerous to be coincidence.

For years I had been crying out for help. I just didn't know it.

23

Starting

1990

My injuries had been explained to me when I had settled on the ward. I had sustained 'multiple bilateral fractures to tibia and fibula' – both legs had been shattered from the knees down. My right heel had taken the initial impact and the brunt of the damage. I had my X-rays explained by a young house doctor who showed me the damage in intricate detail. I had suffered in excess of 50 separate breaks in my right leg and roughly 25 breaks in my left. He told me that I had very little chance of walking again and that I should prepare myself for amputation of my right leg, if not both legs.

Either I didn't fully comprehend the magnitude of what I had been told or I'd already subconsciously worked out what the extent of the damage was, as my reaction was almost passive. No tears, no anger, no histrionics. I was now officially a cripple. This seemed to give my life a context. I was fine with what I had been told.

At least I was when in the company of others.

At that point I had not yet seen my legs; all I knew was that they were bloody sore. After several operations, I was to be transferred to Bangour Village Hospital in West Lothian, a unit that specialised in the treatment of burns. I was to have a series of skin grafts and a muscle-flap procedure. This was to be done in one operation, as it was considered I had already had a dangerous amount of anaesthetic in a short period of time. I was in theatre for most of the day. I must have been given huge amounts of drugs, as I remained sedated until early the following morning.

It was on that morning that I saw my 'new' legs for the very first time. I was appalled by what I was looking at. I almost vomited, such was the impact, but I couldn't bring myself to look away. Not so long ago, I'd had thick, muscular, well-defined footballer's legs. Now I had grotesque, misshapen, scar-ridden stumps. The muscle-flap section of the operation had involved one of my calf muscles being rotated and affixed to the inside of my ankle. The gap left had then been covered by a gossamer-thin piece of skin grafted from my thigh. The other leg showed an angry oval scar, also covered with grafted skin, running half the length of my shin. There were metal staples and countless blue stitches. Both my thighs had lost a lot of muscle and were now very skinny. What the fuck had I done to myself?

I cried unashamedly until the ambulance came to return me to the Royal Infirmary. I lay silently on the stretcher, alone with my thoughts. Thoughts of the horribly mutilated legs that were to be a part of me forever more. Or at least until I had the ugly fuckers cut off.

On arrival back at Ward 2, I was promoted to a bed in a four-berth side ward, a room where the less acute patients were billeted. The first thing that was to be done was the removal of my morphine infusion pump. I was terrified. They were taking away the only thing that was making this bearable. I protested strongly, as the memory of the unbearable pain was all too fresh in my mind. I couldn't deal with that again, not so soon. The staff were adamant. They said I had been on it longer than was necessary and they had to ensure I would not develop dependence. It was to be replaced by four-hourly injections of a slightly higher dose. At that time, I was unaware of the dangers of prescribed opiate addiction but by then it was already too late. They were starting the process of weaning me off the large amounts of diamorphine my body had grown accustomed to. Thankfully, I never did develop a smack habit; codeine was to become my particular drug of choice.

Starting

After being on the side ward for a few weeks, I was to be transferred to the Princess Margaret Rose Orthopaedic Hospital in the south of the city. The PMR had a brilliant reputation for pioneering work in the field of orthopaedics. It was known throughout Europe as the best in its field and to this day is sadly missed by former patients and staff alike.

The regime there was far less stringent than it had been in the Royal Infirmary. While the staff timings, drug rounds, nurse meetings and bed-making were all regular and the routine rarely deviated from, there was a much more relaxed atmosphere, no doubt because this was a hospital dealing with the long, laborious process of healing broken bones. Patients were afforded a lot more leeway as regards how they spent their day. Before long, I was responding well to the treatment and was moved to an even more relaxed regime on a side ward, mainly used to billet people who had suffered the ignominious heartache of amputation. One night, when all was quiet (apart from an elderly chap who was the mandatory heavy snorer), all eight residents in the room were awoken by a loud growl and sharp thudding noise. Scott had been lying awake, getting increasingly annoyed with the snorer's relentless performance, and had snapped. He'd picked up his prosthetic leg and thrown it at Jake, the snorer, hitting him flush on the head. A groggy, disorientated Jake awoke with a start and after a few seconds worked out what had happened. 'What the fuck'd you do that for, ya wee bastard?' he spat across the room (he was capable of little else, as his own false limb was lying on the floor beside his bed). A gormless grin spread across Scott's face just as he replied, deadpan, 'Well, it's ages since I've had my leg over!', much to everyone's mirth – even grumpy old Jake.

Scott had lost his right leg when the motorbike he had been riding was sucked underneath a lorry attempting to overtake him on a dual carriageway. Initially, his was a below-knee amputation but a series of complications and infections meant he had been back to theatre to have more and more of his leg seared off until, eventually, his stump was barely lower than his groin. He deserved all the good luck in the world. Not long after, he was awarded a significant amount of compensation, although he was fairly ambivalent about the whole thing. I have a lasting memory of when he was told about the money, as all he said,

115

in a dispassionate monotone, was, 'It won't make my fucking leg grow back, though, will it?' He had every right to be bitter.

Every weekday, I attended two hours of physiotherapy in a large custom-built gym. I think, looking back, that this was really designed to lift my spirits as much as heal my broken legs and get them working again. All I seemed to do was lift small weights attached to my plaster-clad ankles or sit in my wheelchair at a multi-gym, building up my upper-body strength, although my shoulders and arms had already firmed up significantly in the short time I had been hauling myself around in my crazy wheelchair. Initially, I'd been quite pleased about being put in the wheelchair. I'd been bed-bound until that point and now I had a degree of freedom, but it was during the next stage that things really changed. When I was put into a walking cast, I finally realised that I wasn't going to lose my legs. I found myself being encouraged and inspired by staff and other patients alike.

I fucking would walk again. I would.

As my determination to walk increased, my sense of humour returned and my spirits had indeed been lifted, almost without my noticing. Yes, there still was a lot of pain and tears involved but the blackness had slowly dissipated, at least for a while. I was not to be confident of walking properly but should be able to 'get around' – I had, on paper, entered the world of the permanently disabled.

The physiotherapy continued and I was getting stronger. Six weeks after first being admitted, I was taken to the plaster room to have the cast on my left leg removed and a new, bigger, stronger cast put on my right. My left leg felt weak but not too sore – miraculous, considering the damage I had done. After the technicians had carefully washed and massaged my leg, I put on a training shoe and sock for the first time in what seemed like an eternity. My first step was just around the corner, as I was to learn when a shoe sole was incorporated into the cast on my right leg. I was elated and scared all at once. I'd seen the recent X-rays of my legs and they had shown nothing more than a slushy area of bone tissue held together by the contents of a small hardware store. I had more steelwork than bone tissue: there was no way I could walk on that. Or was there?

I certainly had the will to do so. When I was initially told I would never walk again, my disturbed mind had just accepted this in an apathetic acquiescence. However, over the weeks that followed, as I regained some of my confidence and natural arrogance, I began to think, who won't walk again? While amputation was still very much a real possibility, particularly for my right leg, I dismissed all thoughts of it. Unknown to me, I had, by default, found a focus through which I could channel all my negativity into something positive.

That afternoon in the physiotherapy gym, my stomach lurched into panic when I first set eyes on the obstacle in front of me. To a normal person it was a simple set of parallel bars about four feet apart. To me, sitting rigidly in my chair, it was a mountain. I would have to learn the mechanics of walking all over again but, unlike a toddler who instinctively gets to his feet and takes his first tentative movements, I had to put all my mental as well as physical resources into my steps.

I felt my veins pulsating in my neck as I stared at the parallel bars, psyching myself up as I never had before. Without saying a word, I nodded to the physiotherapists standing on either side of me. I took a deep breath and a look of sheer determination fixed upon my face as my chest swelled fully with the air in my lungs. Slowly, as one, they lifted me from the confines of my chair all the way to my full height.

A sudden rush of blood to my head took me close to passing out and the unused muscles in my lower back protested as they took the weight of my upper body for the first time in six weeks. Trembling, I desperately grabbed the bars on either side of me. At that moment, there seemed to be total silence in the gym. Many of the other patients had got to know me and were aware that I was apparently never to walk again. The rest of the room was still, unmoving, as the others there witnessed my personal battle against the odds; staff and patients alike were holding their collective breath. I relaxed and composed myself, oblivious to the expectant sets of eyes upon me. My physio whispered, 'OK, Jeff, right foot first, easy does it.' I took one step and a new pain coursed all the way up my left leg as my right moved forward. I gulped in more air and the trembling increased. I now had to move my hands from the bars: left hand first, then the right as I moved my left leg forward. My brain had worked out how to walk with the aid of my arms and shoulders. The cast on my right leg, although appearing to be a weight-bearing support, was really designed in such a way as to distribute the majority of my body weight through my knees, thighs and hips. I found my rhythm, slow but progressive, and my buckled body was dragged the full length of the catwalk I was limping along. The physio helped me turn around when I got to the end and I was to attempt the trip back to my chair. While the walk back had at first seemed daunting, it felt quicker. I had done it. Not without some serious help, but I had done it.

I had walked.

24

Miracle

1990

My physical recovery had, so far, gone much better than could ever have been expected, so some form of setback was almost inevitable. After about a week, during doctors' rounds, X-rays were produced which showed that a new fracture had occurred in my right leg. The metal bar had not been strong enough and, as I had built up my walking, the tibia had broken in two, held together by only a few screws. It was a disaster.

For some reason, I always felt intimidated by my consultant and when he told his entourage that I would be back in theatre for yet another operation the following day, I was distraught. I'd had enough surgery to last several lifetimes and I was tired. It wasn't just the actual operation that caused concern but the aftermath – the removal of staples, the dismantling of various drains held in position to the flesh with spiked metal clamps, the dressings sticking to raw flesh, the confinement in bed, the relying on others for everything and, most of all, the lack of freedom.

Some people did ask, when I felt like this, how did I deal with the fact that I had brought all of this on myself. Yes, I had done this to myself but I was seriously disturbed. My suicide attempt hadn't exactly been

119

an informed choice. I never tried to absolve myself of responsibility but how can anyone explain this way of thinking, this way of being, to anyone else who has not crossed that particular line? I had been in such a pit of despair that I had made this – very – serious attempt to simply execute myself, but now I had another objective. My focus had changed and I needed to defy the odds and walk again. This was a goal in itself – the self-analysis would come later.

I was on the theatre list for the next day and yet nobody had the decency to tell me to my face. As I lay sobbing, a nurse broke away from the group surrounding my consultant, who had moved on to another patient. Louise was one of life's genuine, lovely people, a woman who was so obviously born to be a nurse. She was pretty, kind, efficient and patient, counterbalanced with a great sense of humour – somebody I regret not keeping in touch with. In the months ahead, she would choose to travel round the world and wrote to me from several exotic locations but, me being me, I neglected to write back.

Louise had been the only one who noticed my distress and she came over to explain what had happened in more detail. She sat for a while, just talking with me about all sorts of things. We discussed my accident (as my suicide attempt was now being referred to at all times) and she told me that in her opinion, having got to know me quite well, I didn't have the symptoms of a psychiatric illness or disease. She believed that the best way to describe what was wrong with me was an emotional deficiency of some sort. Maybe that over-simplified what had happened to me throughout my life but it made a lot more sense to me than any psychobabble I had listened to from the so-called experts. As I had stumbled through my life from one crisis to another, a void had grown in me where certain emotions should dwell. The emotion I was least equipped to deal with was love, the most important of all. I wanted to love and be loved but I just couldn't get it right. I thought I knew how to love but in reality I was too needy and in the event of believing I had found it, I tried too hard to keep it.

My head was getting stronger and so even the prospect of this next operation was not enough to knock me permanently off-course. The operation to repair the latest damage went well, with no complications at all. I was surprised that I was encouraged to walk with my crutches again eight days afterwards but I rose to the challenge successfully and finally, after three months, two weeks and four days as an in-patient, I was informed I could be discharged. I would walk out on my own two feet. Nothing short of a miracle. Little did I know that the real struggle was just about to begin. The day I walked out of hospital, waving goodbye to my trusty old wonky wheelchair for ever, was the first day of the rest of my life. And what a life it would prove to be.

As part of my recovery, I'd been permitted to spend weekends at my mum's and to begin with I felt fine about being back there. On these weekends, I'd been taken out by friends a few times and met a lot of new people. I was toeing the 'accident' line on the outside and I felt a fraud amongst such sincerely decent folks. My mate Tony was as much responsible for my long-term recovery as any surgeon. He and his friends looked after me without being patronising. As far as they were concerned, I was just a lad who had been unlucky to break his legs; they didn't know the truth. During this period, I began to feel like a normal 21-year-old man. I had all but stopped moping over Leanne, as I had decided there was more to my life than being in a relationship.

Now I was back at my mum's indefinitely and the first day of the rest of my life ended as I lay alone on a put-down bed in the middle of her sitting room. I'd been away from her for around two years and although it was decent of my mother to allow me back, I felt in the way already. We both had to try very hard to get along, and try we did, probably far too hard. It was only a matter of time before the slow-burning fuse edged ever closer to the dynamite.

I'd become institutionalised in hospital, with an army of professionals at my beck and call. It had been easy to take these people for granted but as I lay feeling sorry for myself on my first night back in the real world I fully appreciated just how much had been done for me. Lying amongst the jumble, I felt imprisoned, robbed of my freedom by a cruel twist of fate. Less than 12 hours after leaving hospital, I re-entered the black depths that had been my real home for as long as I could remember. The room I lay in held a lot of bad memories for me and images of my past flashed through my mind. I knew I had made a bad decision in choosing to return to my mum's at such a vulnerable point in my life and I couldn't find the grace to be grateful to her; I was more interested and obsessed with potential areas of future conflict. I had too much hate inside me.

At the time of my jump, I had been unemployed and receiving £26 a week in state benefit. I couldn't realistically return to my bedsit in the north of the city, as the memories would put me back to square one. I'd been due to start a course at a local college the day my adjustment to hospital life had commenced and that had been put on hold indefinitely. To be fair, I had only been going through the motions when I applied and was accepted, as I was completely preoccupied with my relationship with Leanne. All in all, the idea of living my life imprisoned by physical incapacitation back at the shabby shell my mother called home rapidly lost its limited appeal. But it wasn't as if I had many options. There was nothing else for it but to knuckle down. Maybe I'd forgotten what living there was like, but the clutter and the disarray that filled the place got to me from almost the first day.

I hadn't really given much thought to the practicalities before I left hospital. My main concern was how people would judge me, whether they would label me a mental case even though the myth of it all being an 'accident' had taken root. My physical recovery had been the priority for me and my medical team; remarkable as it may seem, the psychiatric side was never addressed. I had been discharged from hospital with a written rehabilitation plan in one hand and a big, blue, sealed polythene bag full of drugs in the other: Triazolam – 0.125mg (30 of, for sleeping), Diclofenac (60 of, for inflammation), Dihydrocodeine or DF118 – 60mg (120 of, for pain), a month's supply of antibiotics and various minerals, vitamins and other dietary supplements. No provision was made for any psychiatric follow-up.

It wouldn't be long before my frustration found an outlet. I'd been in the cramped sitting room for a couple of weeks when I asked my mum if she could clear one of the other rooms so that I could have a bit of space. It would be an odd situation, having a room of my own in that house, but I had resigned myself to sticking around for the long haul.

I was no longer in any state to harm myself, even although shortly after my discharge I had eaten all my sleeping tablets in a petulant outburst at my impotence. This had no effect. I had rapidly developed a tolerance to the drugs due to the huge doses I had been treated with. I was in the early stages of drug use and, despite what I was doing to myself (and had been for some time), I didn't have what might be considered physiological effects. My liver was fine. In fact, I now know that the liver is an extremely resilient organ and that liver damage occurs over a long period of substance abuse. Unless there is an underlying problem, it can take years, sometimes decades, for liver disease to manifest itself – thankfully, given what I've done to mine, I seem to have a particularly good liver.

My mum initially agreed to clear a room for me but, as had always been the case, nothing happened to move things along. After waiting for what I believed was long enough, I took the matter into my own hands. The very hands I needed to get around with. One Friday evening, my mum had gone out with one of her friends and I was alone in the house. The horrors of what I'd done to myself kicked in. I couldn't understand why there was no way out of my shitty life. I'd even failed to kill myself. I humphed my body up to full height with my sticks and moved clumsily across the hallway, heading towards the room opposite the living room.

Looking at the clock, I reckoned I had around three hours before my mum returned. I had to work fast. I pushed experimentally at the door of the room. It didn't budge more than a couple of inches. When I finally stumbled through the gap and put the light on, my jaw dropped. The room that only a few years before had been the best in the house had in the intervening period been relieved of its duties as the 'lounge'. I couldn't see as much as a square inch of floor space. No end of miscellaneous junk was stacked in a mountainous, dust-powdered heap from the skirting boards inwards. Where to start? Making a clearing if able-bodied would have been hard enough. I should have given up there and then. But I had an urge to prove something. I would clear a space on the floor at least, a space in which I could sleep, even if it killed me.

I got a foothold in between a bin bag full of rags and a big, dark-

123

brown, heavy-looking wardrobe. Working myself into a frenzy, I picked up the ragbag and on one leg and one crutch launched it into the hall. I then turned to face the small wooden cabinet that was preventing the door from opening fully and swept the crap away from its surface with a crutch. With one arm, I attempted to lift it away from its position adjacent to the door but couldn't. Sweat started pouring as I braced myself for another go. Still it wouldn't budge. In a flash of rage-inspired revelation, I dropped to my knees, leaving my sticks propped up against the wall beside me, and shuffled closer to the wee innocent-looking cabinet. This time, with much more purchase afforded my upper body, it came away easily. I picked it up as best I could and, still on my knees, half-dragged, half-carried it round the door and threw it into the hall, where its landing was cushioned by the ragbag. The space it had taken up now gave me a starting point.

I heaved, dragged, pushed and pulled all manner of things around the room until I happened across a full-length dressing mirror that was stuck fast under a larger piece of heavy furniture beside it. I tugged at it to no avail, all the while becoming more and more enraged. That was the moment when I lost what little self-control I had left as I saw a deformed, twisted cripple staring back at me. The visible scars on my body glowed crimson through the rivulets of sweat streaming down from my naked shoulders and chest; my ugly, ugly face, contorted with pain and the effort of my exertions, disgusted me. I never hated anyone so much as I hated the man in the mirror.

I found a new strength from somewhere deep inside and, with a hellish roar, picked up the object that had forced me to look at my true self and hurled it across the room. The wooden support and frame snapped apart as glass shards rained down.

I then set about wrecking the entire contents of the room. Every piece of junk was destroyed until there was nothing left intact. I smashed, ripped, shattered and demolished everything in that room. Eventually, I had made a clearing of sorts with a heap of broken furniture, smashed ornaments and torn fabric piled high to one side in a mound almost reaching to the ceiling. I sat, spent, catching my breath amongst the shards of glass and wooden splinters, blood oozing from the cuts now stinging my flesh. I cried, the tears drying as soon as I heard the key in the door announcing the return of my mother.

Tears or no tears, I was still buzzing from my perceived victory and I got myself to my feet, where I stood unaided when my mum passed the doorway and initially failed to notice anything amiss. Since I had jumped, we'd both been walking on eggshells around each other but something had to give. My performance was just the thing to restore hostilities. I noticed an expression of fear shoot across her features. It was gone as quickly as it had appeared and was replaced with a fixed stare of defiance. Cripple or not, there was no way I could see her accepting my destruction of her property. As far as I was concerned, I would give as good as I got, if not better. I had long since lost the fear I once had of my mother physically and she knew it. She could still inflict untold pain on me with words, though, and I knew it.

'Fuckin' say something, woman!' I roared into the silence. When I realised she wasn't going to reply, I picked up the first piece of broken furniture that was to hand and threw it directly at her. And then another. And another. It wasn't until most of the junk pile had been significantly depleted that I noticed my mother had gone. Throwing stuff out of my way, I fell to my knees, my legs finally giving up, and I crawled into the hall and saw the back door lying wide open. With new cuts opening all over my body as I moved, I felt only an exhilarating, overwhelming sense of victory.

I had won. Hadn't I?

25

Need

1991–93

I had taken to sleeping during the day and began to lead a nocturnal life. I've always had an irrational problem dealing with noise, even trivial background sounds that bypass most people, and so night-time suited me better – the quiet was one of the many attractions. My mum and I kept our distance from each other but in the wake of my one-man demolition performance she, to her eternal credit, had purchased for me a brand-new single bed. I'd struggle with daytime, particularly mornings (unless they were seamlessly connected to the night before), for the rest of my life. If I wasn't out, I'd lie awake reading.

The year 1991 began as its predecessor had ended. I continued to spend most of my time during the day asleep, assisted by prescribed medication, and stayed out till all hours at night. It would prove to be a good year for me, one of my happiest, as my rehabilitation would exceed all expectations. Sexually, I embarked upon a series of meaningless one-night stands, never turning down the opportunity of a sympathy shag.

Nine months after being set in plaster, and seven since I had started using crutches, I was finally able to walk unaided. I still needed a walking stick to help with balance but I relied on it more to rebuild my public confidence.

The arguments with my mother had all but stopped, as we now lived almost separate lives under the same roof: her by day and me by night. She had even relaxed her rule of not permitting people to come into the house. On the many occasions when my pain (which would always be significant) got the better of me and I was virtually bed-bound, one of my mates would come round and sit well into the early morning. Mum was actually nice to a lot of them, often being charming, welcoming and even on occasion a tad coy with a select few. This was as much a new experience for her as it was for me, the house sometimes being overrun with a procession of young blokes who had the good grace to ignore the surroundings my mother and I lived in.

When my walking stick got its marching orders, I was living life to the hedonistic max. Against the most heavily stacked odds, I was walking again on my own two feet, albeit with the assistance of some seriously powerful drugs, and only with the slightest of limps. I still experienced episodes of deep, black, contemplative self-analysis but these were becoming fewer and further between as even I was impressed with the remarkable progress I had made. But I was still getting no psychiatric help.

I had enrolled on a four-year degree course, my place being generously held over from the previous year when I had been too preoccupied to commence, but this was something that, like most other things in my life, I failed to complete. I never seemed to have any staying power, something inside arresting the urge to conclude any project or task I set myself. I was capable, of that there was no doubt, but intellectual ability is never enough on its own.

College was, however, a tremendous place for meeting women and my extended shag-fest went from strength to strength. It was at this time I really came into my own in terms of sexual promiscuity, although I still found myself getting just a tad too emotionally involved with one or two girls I went out with. I would get to know them, have some decent sexual encounters with them and then rapidly find myself fantasising about making a future with them. It would be at that point that I would check myself and pull back. If I had learned anything during my ruinous liaisons with women, it was that sex and love were most definitely not interchangeable. And anyway, I was enjoying myself way too much to let emotional weakness get in the way of a half-decent shag!

By mid-1991, my life had become one of extreme decadence. As well as my benefits, which I continued to receive as a student, I started working part-time on Saturdays in a job that would prove to be lucrative for many years. For legal reasons, I can't go into any detail about where this job was or what exactly it entailed but all that mattered to me was that, at the start, I got an extra £15 in my hand for an easy day's work. Money wasn't a problem and so I was also drinking fairly heavily. I took the party life very seriously, slowly developing a reputation as a hard drinker, usually the last to leave at the end of the night, always looking to go on somewhere else to satisfy my huge capacity for alcohol.

Eventually, I dropped out of college and started to pursue my hedonistic lifestyle on a full-time basis. In the summer of 1992, I popped into the pub to watch one of the Euro 92 football matches on the big screen, hoping to happen across someone I could tap a few quid off until my benefit was paid later in the week. I sat in the larger of the two corner bays, quietly nursing a glass of orange juice, head down in concentration on one of the Sunday papers' prize crosswords. I hardly noticed when I was joined in the corner by two young women, only one of whom I knew. I nodded in recognition but went back to my crossword, occasionally glancing up at the telly.

Claire had always been on the periphery of the company and she and I had shared a brief flirtation the previous year that came to nothing. We bore each other no ill will, however, putting it down to experience, and it was with ease that we chatted away when the crossword finally stumped me.

Her friend, Rebekah (or 'wee Rebekah' as she was apparently known, no doubt down to the fact she stood just over five foot), was obviously painfully shy and remained quiet and still, not moving a muscle as Claire and I spoke to each other across her. Rebekah was small, chubby and almost boyish, with big, brown doe-eyes underneath a shock of wavy brown hair cut close at the back and sides. Through the layers of make-up, I could see she had the remnants of what were obviously teenage acne scars but they paled into insignificance when she emitted a brief laugh at one of my many inane comments. When she smiled, she lit the room up as she revealed a set of large, beautifully formed, perfectly even, clean, white teeth. It was a smile that demanded an RSVP. She looked very young: under the make-up, I guessed she was no more than 16. With her boyish looks and baggy clothes, I immediately thought that she was a lesbian and paid her little attention (in terms of her being a potential conquest – such was my attitude at the time) as she helped me fill in the blanks in the crossword I was continuing to trouble over.

As it would turn out, this mousey wee lassie would develop an unprecedented talent for 'filling in the blanks', particularly those blanks I would trouble over in the future. And while her shyness was very real at the time, this demure, well-spoken, dove-like creature would show herself to have nerves of steel and a huge, loving, forgiving heart. She would need them, that's for sure.

Not that I would notice these qualities for many years to come. As she slid the pen from out of my grasp and completed the puzzle with consummate ease (the answer being 'elevate', which is ironic, given what the future would hold), I didn't know that I had just met my wife for the very first time.

It was three or four months later before I would bump into Rebekah again. As I left the toilets in a busy uptown bar, she was standing to one side right outside the door, holding a drink in each hand. Initially, we didn't recognise each other. She looked really pretty that night and because she carried a bit of excess timber I considered her to be just within my reach. Before much longer, both of us had lost our respective pals and were kissing.

On that first night, I saw Rebekah as nothing more than another potential addition to my growing collection of one-night stands. We moved on to a nearby club and then got a taxi to my mum's house. I couldn't put my finger on it but I did feel a closeness with Rebekah even at that early stage. However, I was unable to express it properly. Though I found Rebekah enchanting, I was still very reluctant to involve myself in a relationship of any importance. That night, however, she did become another metaphorical notch in the bedpost. If I thought that the sex was anything but memorable I was to be proved very, very wrong.

Over the next month or so, we saw quite a lot of one another. She was growing on me, although apart from that first night we had not taken the sexual side of our developing relationship any further. I was happy enough to continue seeing her without having sex, at least for the time being. She had become in such a short time more than any girlfriend I'd had before. She became my friend. I thought the sex thing would sort itself out in time and I didn't want to destroy this friendship because of what was a minor issue. I was happy to wait. Within reason.

I was falling in love properly for the very first time. I was ready for it. I was so very near to the love that I had searched for all my life. Love for its own sake, not based on sex but on companionship, romance, frivolity and fun. The kind of love that had evaded me all my life was so close it was palpable, until I heard two life-changing words.

'I'm pregnant,' she said.

Cue the most stupid of questions ever to be asked.

'But how?' said I, the erstwhile student of the female reproductive system. She looked sheepishly up at me, her eyes moist and emanating vulnerability, apologising: apologising for being pregnant, her voice little more than a whisper. At that moment, I could only think of myself. I am ashamed to admit that in an instant I became self-absorbed and totally arrogant. I said very little but inside I resented her; I blamed her. All I could see before me was yet another woman hell-bent on destroying whatever happiness I had in my life. Just like all the rest. Just like my mum: my mum who had, shock of all shocks, decided that she liked Rebekah, really liked her. They were fucking welcome to each other. I was devastated. Instead of concerning myself with Rebekah's helpless plight and general wellbeing, all I could think of was me, me, me.

Rebekah was a frightened, weakened, isolated girl of only 20, whose life had been turned upside down because of one night with me, and I didn't care. I turned away and looked out over the green expanse of Holyrood Park, collecting my thoughts, trying to come up with an acceptable response. I remained mute, wishing she would just get back in her car and go away, away anywhere but close to me.

'I don't know what to say,' I said pathetically, looking at her with barely concealed malevolence. She held my gaze but only until the hint of tears began to form in the corner of her big, brown, saddened eyes. She folded herself carefully into the driver's seat of her dark maroon car and turned the key in the ignition. Before she turned her head to face the windscreen and drive away down the slope of St Leonard's Lane, we shared another, more pertinent, more telling, fleeting look. Our lives were now intrinsically linked but not in the way either of us had hoped for only a few weeks before.

But none of that mattered to me then. I was now eight months away from becoming the one thing I truly never wanted to be. A father.

A few months into her pregnancy, Rebekah was offered voluntary redundancy, which made the decision to become a full-time mum much easier. While our relationship continued, my heart was no longer in it, even though I had accepted we would now be connected for ever. We still saw a lot of each other, despite the change in dynamic, but it was mainly at her house, where she lived with her parents and elderly grandmother. I couldn't get past the fact that she had become pregnant on the first and only occasion we'd had sex. I was bitter about the whole thing and kept up my behaviour as a man about town, but the relationship continued and I felt it was important that I remained faithful to her. I had always had a thing about monogamy: I believed it was fundamentally wrong to indulge in infidelity, even though my best friend Ross, who had taken up the best-mate baton from Tony, was an accomplished adulterer, behaviour I would lambast him for on many an occasion. I had met Ross in early October 1990 through Tony – I had only known him a short while at this point but he was to become one of the three best friends I've ever had.

As Rebekah's pregnancy developed, our relationship became as good as platonic and, on my part, distant. The more remote I tried to become from Rebekah, the more determined she was to make it work. I was curt with her, and sometimes downright nasty, but still she remained stoic and loyal to me, often lending me some cash or visiting me at home when I was recovering from a minor operation to remove some metalwork from my right leg in January 1993. She brought me gifts, even buying me my first-ever computer game, and sent me cards with tender words and genuine heartfelt messages. Never once did I reciprocate, always harking back to the time when *she* got pregnant, as if I'd been nothing more than a passing spectator. I was awful to her but she loved me. There was no intimacy or tenderness between us, purely because of my behaviour. It was only a matter of time before what remained of our relationship crumbled and it was to come crashing down just three months before the birth of our baby. I was again in the midst of spiralling out of control and unable to really see just how much real love was within my grasp, so once again I applied my finger to that big red self-destruct button.

This time it happened after a Sunday-night drinking session in my local, when a group of us headed into town. We ended up in a downmarket nightclub, all sparkly spinning balls and sticky carpets. My heart almost leapt out of my chest when I set eyes on Cath – it was the first time I had seen her since I'd hurt her five years before. The alcohol gave me a false sense of courage and while I'd been terrified of this meeting ever happening, I could handle it now. Having lived with Cath during what was a tempestuous time for us both, I knew that we were not a good mix. But I still considered her to be my first proper love, although I now concede that she was no more than my first real girlfriend. We had little to show for that year of madness – a burst face for her and a criminal conviction for me. We got chatting and left the club. Walking up Lothian Road with a hostile but chatty Cath, a relationship with anyone was the furthest thing from my mind.

Old times' sake has a nasty habit of being used as an excuse for lots of things.

26

Love

27 JULY 1993

I'm clad in surgical green from head to toe. The white wooden clogs I wear tap an irregular beat as I limp across the highly polished floor into the centre of the startlingly bright floodlit room where Rebekah lies, passive and bloated on the raised platform. I'm ushered to a stool that has been placed to the side of her right shoulder, which protrudes slightly over the side of the narrow mattress she lies on.

She looks beautiful but the darkened hue of the taut skin around her big brown eyes indicates exhaustion. There is a droplet of moisture in one of mine as I try to focus on feeling the way I know I should. She turns her head towards me and I can almost taste the fear. She has the look of an innocent farm animal who has just realised it is to be slaughtered. I know she loves me and I should admit how my heart feels about her, but it is so long since I told the truth or admitted anything that I don't know where to start.

As I look down, over her shoulder, her tiny hand clenches mine in time with the slight movement noticeable from under the suspended white sheet held above, concealing the space her swollen belly fills.

Another anonymous green shape stands poised with a shiny weapon and applies it to the place we cannot see. There is much movement and concentration all around us as something life-changing happens.

Our eyes meet again and I see that the look of fear has intensified in her eyes. I look deep into them and feel something move inside me (love? Is that what it is?) but I push it back before it can express itself. I, too, am frightened. I know she loves me, loves me more than anyone ever has, but I fight the urge to accept her love. Even here. Even now. I want to love her back but at this time, in this place, I resist the impulse to relinquish the hold I think I have over it, the relinquishment of love.

I am distracted by a familiar yet unique sound coming from the direction of the green man with the blade. He has put aside the shiny steel implement and in its place is the gore-encrusted creature responsible for the alien sound. It is a sound that has irritated and enraged me to the point of despair throughout my life, yet now, right now, as the screaming creature is placed at the breast of Rebekah, I love it. I love the creature. The creature is my son. I love his mother. She is my redemption. I love her. I love him. I love me. I love life.

I love.

I cannot love.

Immediately, I close my heart. As I hold my son and look at him, I'm proud but sorry. I'm so scared. I look at his mother but she won't look at me. She can sense what I am feeling, what I am thinking. I have yet to recognise that she really is my angel and so I refuse to be guided. My life has changed for ever but I didn't plan this change. I didn't want this change. I resent this change.

I sit but the love has gone. It is back in its safe place where it cannot be seen. I will not let it out. I hold my son and am strangely comforted by his tiny fragile body as he sleeps in the crook of my arm. I am confused. A voice from somewhere deep inside me tells me that this is a good thing but I ignore it. I know better. I always know better.

I place the delicate bundle gently in his mother's arms, the place I know he really belongs, and as I do so, I kiss both their foreheads lightly with my dry lips. I turn away from them and I walk.

I walk aimlessly through the streets and ponder life in my new role. I have a chance to change my life for the better but I know I cannot cope with change. I see a chance at last to love and be loved, yet I pass up that chance because, when everything is stripped bare, I know in my heart that I do not deserve to be loved. I am not worthy of unquestioning love. Instead, I will resent.

I will resent myself.

I will resent the woman I love.

And I will resent my son.

27

Coming Around Again

1993–94

I walked out of the Simpson Memorial Maternity Pavilion on that wet Tuesday evening on which Daniel was born to go home. Another home. Not one I shared with the woman who had just given birth to my child. Home was now Lothian Road, which was at that time the epicentre of the city's nightlife. I'd been sharing a bedsit with Cath and had convinced myself that we were worth another go. I had 'officially' ended my relationship with Rebekah before she gave birth. She was seven months pregnant, vulnerable, afraid and very much in love with her baby's father, and she had just been dumped. Rebekah had been so nice to me since she had fallen pregnant with our child and all I could do was retreat back inside my selfish shell, adopting an air that would kindly be described as cold and aloof. As far as I was concerned, she was to blame for this position I was now in and that was the end of it.

When Daniel was just weeks old, Rebekah agreed to allow me to have him on Monday, Wednesday and Friday mornings. I was blissfully unaware of the mammoth task I had let myself in for. No wonder Rebekah looked knackered. I had a romanticised idea that babies just slept, had the odd bottle of milk and gurgled away in the corner. After

136

the first few occasions when I was left alone with my son, it became clear that I couldn't cope.

I began to strongly dislike the boy, really dislike him. It was five months into Daniel's life when I knew I had to put my hands up and admit defeat. He had a bad morning and just wouldn't stop screaming, his constant wailing cutting right through me, winding me up further and further. In a blind rage, I picked him up and roared at him to 'Shut up, please just fucking shut up.' It was the ensuing short, empty silence that brought me back down. In that interlude, the red mist evaporated and I began sobbing as I held my child, who was now crying louder than ever, close to me. Hating myself for what I knew I could have done, I gathered Daniel up and took him across the road with me to the phone box and called his mother, asking her to come and collect him after explaining what had happened. She was there within the half hour and as I watched the maroon Ford Escort edge away through the heavy city-centre traffic, I knew that I had been close, too close, to doing something terrible.

My relationship with Cath had reverted to type, with very violent arguments interspersed with conciliatory, angry bouts of sex. Even though I should have known much better by then, I was still viewing sex and love as interchangeable. I had transferred my need for love onto a need for sex. The better the sex became, the more I thought I was loved and therefore in love.

Cath and I just grated on each other's nerves and it got worse as we were now sharing only one room. I was full of good intentions but before long the arguments resumed, then the lacerating personal insults until the taunts of abusive bravado eventually descended into fists being thrown all over the place. I lost my temper too easily with Cath, as she had become both my physical and emotional punchbag.

Around this time, I had taken to using the over-the-counter drug diphenhydramine hydrochloride, an antihistamine with strong sedative properties. Using soon became abusing and within a short period of time I was very rarely in an alert state of consciousness, sometimes sleeping for up to 18 hours a day. While Cath was used to my nocturnal habits, she soon got sick of me sleeping my life away on the couch, then crawling into bed beside her, where I would stay till she returned from her job in the early evenings. Inevitably, we would argue, then fight, then I would hurt her and then be sorry. Afterwards, we would make up in the only way we knew how, before the whole sorry cycle would start all over again.

One night, as she lay on the bed and I sat on the couch, Cath asked me what should have been a harmless everyday question in the middle of a conversation we were having. 'Have you got any secrets that you've never told to a soul?' she enquired. My quick answer was, 'No, I don't think so, nothing bad anyway. Why do you ask?' She went on to recount a tale of innocent sexual teenage exploration. The conversation resumed and that, I believed, was the end of it.

Over the course of the following few weeks, however, her words haunted me, infiltrating my every thought. 'Have you got any secrets?', 'Any secrets?', 'Secrets?', over and over in my head. 'No!' 'No!' 'No!' 'No!'

One night, as I wandered through the Meadows alone, the words came back again.

'Got any secrets?'

'No!'

Pause.

Stop dead.

And then the voice of the demons, 'Oh yes, you fucking have!!!!!'

The good old boys were back, bigger and better and more cunning than they had ever been.

Overnight, my drug abuse increased, as I needed to run further away than I ever had in the past. I slept for as long as I could and when I could sleep no more I took more drugs. If Cath noticed, she never mentioned it, preferring to attack the consequences rather than the cause. The fighting resumed with a new edge to it. My assaults on her became more frenzied, until finally she could take no more. I had stopped caring about anything, not even making a token effort with Daniel. I was a waster, an unemployed layabout who spent his days in his pit.

The demons were coming. The foggiest of memories ascended slowly to the surface: an image of a big, fat, hairy man flitting in and out of focus, an image that began to dominate my drug-induced sleep with ever-increasing clarity. There was something real about him. Something bad, something savage, as he laughed at me, taunting me. I would wake up soaking with perspiration brought on by the chemicals and the pure evil that had been unleashed from its cage deep within me.

One evening, as I sat nursing my anger, I deliberately provoked an argument with Cath. Predictably enough, it escalated into a full-scale fight, with me slapping her all over the room we shared. Eventually, I pushed her onto the couch and she fell, lengthways, onto her back, one arm dangling over onto the floor. We were screaming abuse at each other viciously as I sat astride her. She bit, scratched and kicked out at me, but my weight and size gave me the physical advantage and before long her breathing shallowed as I crushed against her chest. She had little option but to calm down and as she did so she hurled a torrent of almost-whispered abuse at me – and that was the moment I crossed the line, if I hadn't done so already.

As my slaps became more frequent, I lost my grip on her throat and she sat up immediately, gasping but with a new-found strength. She grabbed at my belt, opened her legs and screamed in my face, 'What are you fucking going to do now then, big man? Fucking rape me?'

I froze.

Rape.

How dare she use that word? I'm not like him. I'm not a rapist.

'Rape!' The word reverberated round and round until my fist impacted on her jawbone. I hated her (him).

I felt nothing. No guilt, no remorse, no pain. Nothing at all. The madness I had been running from throughout my childhood years had teamed up with a stranger and caught up with me. The madness had forced a way in and had every intention of staying put for the long haul.

When I returned to the bedsit, Cath had gone. Quite rightly so. I felt guilty and alone but even after what I had done I still blamed her. She had now abandoned me. Rejected me. Again.

Never having lived alone before, not properly alone, I found it impossible to adjust. This was my first real experience of the sour taste of loneliness. Filled with guilt and self-loathing, I was alone with the demons that danced inside me, who seemed stronger than ever before. Alone with the madness that I thought I had left behind when I jumped out of that top-flat window almost four years earlier. Now they had found me again and I had dues to pay.

Feeling abandoned and rejected, I poured my heart out to Rebekah as she sat on the edge of my grubby bed with our son. She took control and in her quietly determined manner set about picking up the pieces of my life and painstakingly putting them back together. She took me out for the day, driving all three of us in her Escort down the coastal road to North Berwick.

I still can't remember how I got there but that same evening, a Monday at the beginning of April 1994, I was admitted as an in-patient to the Royal Edinburgh Hospital, sometimes referred to as the Andrew Duncan Clinic but known throughout the city as 'the loony bin'. Within a few hours of my arrival, I felt something foreign but uplifting wash all over me. As I got my bearings on the ward, I noticed how different it was to the frantic movement I had experienced in mainstream hospitals. I felt so safe, safe and warm – despite the superficially tatty surroundings with paint peeling from the walls, making way for the thick layers of tobacco stains. I knew I was in the right place.

My initial consultation with the duty psychiatrist had been very calm as I told him I had been sliding badly, overwhelmed by the memories of that night in 1987 that had come flooding back and added to the layers of pain. I described the recent events that had culminated in me presenting myself at the hospital in a desperate act that was a more practical cry for help than the suicide I so dearly wanted to commit. As soon as the words 'abuse' and 'rape' were uttered, the dynamic of the interview changed dramatically and I was admitted to the hospital immediately.

Having been put on close observation, I would be monitored constantly and denied permission to leave the ward alone, which meant there was little I could do other than light up a cigarette and reflect upon the life that had brought me to this place. I had previously attended the young persons unit in a different area of the grounds of this hospital after having been confidentially referred by my house teacher when in my fifth year at school. She had also been my English teacher and had seen something dark in some of the things I had written, something that alarmed her enough to have me checked out. In the event, I managed to bluster my way through a few out-patient appointments, very aware of the stigma that goes along with mental-health issues. And so, after spinning a few strategically placed lies and reticent silences, at 16 years old I had been written off with a clean bill of mental health. Nine years later, on that Monday night, for the first time in months, I drifted off into a deep sleep without anything chemical to send me on my way.

I spent the first 72 hours on the ward, as I remained under close observation. Initially, I feared I had been sectioned but after it had all been explained clearly to me – that it was normal practice for first-time in-patients to be watched so closely but I could, if I wanted, discharge myself at any time – I was satisfied that I was in a place that could help me. I stayed.

With little alternative, I spent the majority of the first three days talking my issues over with the staff or thinking about my life and my need to bring my own death forward. The three days of interviews and self-analysis came and went, and when I was told I could go off the ward without an escort I found, surprisingly, that my general mood had lifted significantly. I hadn't found my answers but I had at least scratched the surface. The staff had been quietly supportive and gently encouraging as they extracted some of my many neuroses.

However, I didn't give up everything.

One thing that remained private was my misuse of the over-the-counter sleepers. I didn't see it as a problem at all, believing that I was in control of the situation. The sleeping tablets were just another method I employed to speed up the clock and run away from my life. It would be a drug of a different type that would eventually drive me into freefall a few years down the line. In the meantime, the sleeping tablets would be the key to the door that opened up my safety zone; they kept some of my problems hidden.

From that time onwards, it would be more than a decade before I would take the normal dose, prescribed, purchased or procured,

141

of any drug that I used; even non-addictive, mundane drugs such as paracetamol, ibuprofen and aspirin would be abused. The sleepers were the first step on my road to a very serious, highly toxic over-the-counter painkiller problem that would ultimately result in my losing everything of any importance. At the time, though, I was an in-patient in the Royal Ed and there were no such concerns. I took the drug to sleep, to sleep longer than I needed to, and that was as much as I cared about.

An addict? Me?

Never.

As soon as I was trusted to sign myself in and out of the ward, I walked into Boots the Chemist and purchased the familiar wee blue box of my favourite night-time sleep aid. It was more luck than anything else that prevented me from damaging my body further, as I had also been prescribed Prozac to deal with my apparent depression as well as large doses of ibuprofen to combat the constant pain in my legs.

During my one-to-one counselling sessions, I opened up about certain things but remained doggedly silent regarding others. I talked at length about the sexual assault, the self-hatred and suicidal urges but I would never revisit my childhood, the 'outsider' complex I had cultivated or the details of my self-harming. While I recognised that the people in hospital were there to help me, I couldn't be totally candid with them. I was ashamed, embarrassed and downright terrified of being judged, so I kept many of the more sordid, painful parts of my life to myself.

When I began to mix with the other patients on the ward, my eyes were opened as I saw at very close quarters just what psychiatric illness was really about. I was at the lower end of the scale. There were people who suffered with an inner torment that even I couldn't begin to imagine.

I was moved into the main part of the ward after my initial period of observation and began to integrate quite well with some of the other patients. They, like me, had travelled long and often painful journeys. Some were veterans of the hospital and some were virgins. Because the regime on the ward was relaxed, no one seemed to bother that my nocturnal body clock had returned to type and often I wouldn't emerge from my bed until lunchtime. Hospital or not, mornings remained anathema to me as I continued to abuse my smuggled stash of sleeping pills.

Although still hung-up about the end of my relationship with Cath and struggling to come to terms with the abuse in my past, after a fortnight on the ward it was decided that I was well enough to be discharged. With nowhere to go, the hospital social worker organised a short-term stay for me in a bed and breakfast back in Leith. Immediately, feelings of fear and isolation kicked in. In the real world, I was a 25-year-old father – running back to Mummy wasn't an option this time.

28

Furies and Demons

1994

After being discharged, I made my way on a number 16 bus to my new temporary address in a street adjacent to Leith Links. On arrival, I was met by a very severe middle-aged woman who, before even showing me to my room, recited the long list of house rules. I switched off after the part that informed me that I would not be permitted on the premises between 10 a.m. and 6 p.m. on weekdays and 10 a.m. and 4 p.m. at weekends. Immediately, I started to panic. What was I to do during the day? Where could I go? I felt alone and vulnerable, having just left a place of safety and security, and now I had to spend my days wandering the streets. I was terrified, anxious and, as the events of the next 24 hours were to prove, nowhere near mentally well enough to be on the streets fending for myself. A chance encounter with my recently assaulted ex-girlfriend would ensure I would not spend even one night in Hotel Nazi.

I'd been walking around the busy Leith streets near the foot of the Walk when I decided to head out to the place from where I had jumped and smashed my legs four years previously. I cannot explain my reasons for wanting to go back there: perhaps it was just a case of something to do, revisiting somewhere familiar, or perhaps I had some distorted idea of attempting to exorcise a few ghosts. In the event, however, I never made it, my legs unable to walk the distance. I got on the first bus that came along and as I sat, head against the window, obsessing miserably about Cath and what had happened to our relationship, who should get on a mile or so along the road? In all the time I had known her, Cath had never had any connections with the area of the city we now found ourselves travelling through. She sat down beside me and chatted away as if nothing had happened, with me ever aware of the faint but noticeable signs of the damage I had done still visible beneath her expertly applied make-up. I kept my eyes well away from meeting hers. With nothing much else in my not-so-busy appointment diary, I stayed on the bus as it headed uptown, back in the direction of Morningside, from where I had come that morning and where Cath had found a new job in an old-folks care home.

When she got off the bus, I followed and now free from the social constraints of the busy bus on its way further south towards Oxgangs and beyond, the conversation took a darker, more heated turn. She was shouting at me to leave her alone, as I trailed behind her all the way to her new place of employment. The tightness in my stomach had given way to a histrionic display of tearful remorse but she was having none of it. Eventually, she was screaming at me to fuck off and that was when I grabbed her shoulders and pleaded with her to try again. As she moved to turn away, half-sneering, half-pitying, the whole world seemed to stop for a microsecond as I punched her square in the eye. I had reverted to type. With Cath. Again. She didn't flinch a bit but just shook her head wearily and entered the massive double wooden doors of the old-folks home. What the fuck had I done?

Already feeling useless and worthless, the guilt-ridden self-loathing that overcame me after this latest, and what was thankfully to prove final, assault on the woman I thought I loved, seemed to narrow my options even further. There were no excuses. I had hurt her again, so, true to form, I would have to turn the physical pain back onto myself. Although I blamed myself, there was also a part of me that blamed her and so, using my fucked-up logic, I decided to show her just what she had done. My self-worth was at an all-time low, so nothing mattered to me apart from what I wanted to be a final, dramatic act of self-destruction. I would make her feel as guilty as I felt. She would be made to feel my pain, the pain I believed she had caused, when I branded an indelible image of my dying body into her mind's eye.

I returned to Leith and sat on a bench in the Links, descending into a fury of self-hatred as I psyched myself up to commit my ultimate act of public self-annihilation. My death wish had not abated as my discharge from hospital might have suggested and having been abandoned (as I saw it) by that self-same hospital that very morning and rejected indubitably once again by Cath, I now planned to commit suicide with the employment of several contingencies.

With the money I had left in my pocket, I purchased a pack of razor blades (safety ones, of course, can't have any unwanted accidents happening!), several boxes of sleeping tablets from various chemist shops, a litre bottle of vodka from Vickie Wines, a thick, blue nylon tow-rope from a service station and a set of stainless steel police-issue handcuffs from the Army and Navy stores just down from Elm Row. My plan was to consume the drink and drugs, slash my wrists and then hang myself from a tree in the grounds of the old-folks home where Cath now worked. The cuffs were to be used to secure my hands behind my back in order to prevent me reaching up and grabbing hold of the rope in the event that I chickened out whilst hanging suspended from my neck. I put a great deal of fucked-up thought into this but the plans of much more efficient and stable people than me have been scuppered and so it was inevitable that my blaze of glory was doomed to failure from the start.

As nightfall enveloped the city, I made my way back to Morningside with my suicide kit safely ensconced in the sturdy Victoria Wine carrier bag dangling innocently from my right hand. I found somewhere quiet and relatively secluded, away from any serial curtain-twitchers who could stop my determined intentions getting past first base. I poured the contents of the ten packets of pills into the big bottle of alcohol and started swigging greedily from it, not acknowledging the bitter, sharp, burning sensation searing down my throat. As the mixture started to take effect, I slid a blade from its plastic sheath and made a tentative

146

cut in my left wrist, just below a previously self-administered scar, and then switched the blade into my left hand and slashed a very deep perpendicular cut in my right. While the blood from my left side flowed freely, dripping steadily onto the ground, my right wrist was spurting blood intermittently, as if someone was turning a tap on and off in time with my heartbeat.

Simultaneously, a thin, almost invisible jet of watery blood was spraying powerfully in the direction I held my arm and I was fascinated by this as I gulped down large mouthfuls of the corrupted vodka. By this time, my perception was heavily clouded but, staggering towards the final leg of my journey, I saw that no matter how hard I had tried to be positive in my life, it had always amounted to this: be it private moments of self-harm or dramatic public displays of self-obliteration, the sad, pathetic truth was that I simply, without really understanding why, despised myself. Despised myself so absolutely that I could see no escape. The one person I could not escape was myself: twenty-four hours a day, seven days a week – every week. I had to live alongside the one person I hated and I couldn't run away indefinitely. It was a horrible conundrum and one that would consume me for a long, long time. Even when I felt happy, there always seemed to be something missing, and when I found somebody who loved me, for me, unconditionally, I would be unable to accept it and instead throw that love away. Even now I do not know why I refuse to be saved from myself by people I know dearly love me. Perhaps the self-hatred is a perverse safety zone that is comfortable because it is familiar, or perhaps I am unable to actually recognise real, worthy love until it's too late and even if I do, I find myself feeling that I am unworthy of it.

Whatever the answer, if indeed the answer is out there, even love is unable to remove the perpetual torment that is as much a part of me as my shadow, torment that I, in the final analysis, invariably seem to create for myself as I consistently grab misery from the jaws of contentment.

That night, clutching the rope in a blood-soaked, cuffed hand, I stood forlornly in the grounds of the old-folks home, shouting incoherently at my ex, who I knew was inside. A matronly woman appeared at the door and told me to go away or she would call the police. I didn't give a fuck about the police and stood my ground, a pool of blood forming at my feet as I continued to shout after my ex, shattering the silence in the otherwise cool, still, cloudless, star-spattered night. Cath appeared from behind the bulk of the woman, her eye now swollen with the badge of a relationship that really never was, and calmly said that she had no feelings left for me any more. The fact that I had harmed myself, she said, made no difference. She quietly told me that it would be better all round if I was just to go. I nodded back in the affirmative, apologised and turned away, the blood spraying from my arm marking the path I had to follow. Through the haze of the drink, drugs and accelerating blood loss, I did what I was told. I went.

I was picked up nearby, still grasping the sticky rope, lying prostrate and semi-conscious in the middle of the road, by the police, who delivered me, well fucked and bleeding badly, to the Royal Infirmary, where I was stitched and admitted overnight before being transferred back up the road, for the last time in this series of events, to the Royal Edinburgh. I had been away less than 24 hours and in that period I had done more damage than most people do in a lifetime, most of it just half a mile or so away, just around the corner.

On the morning I was re-admitted, the place appeared silent to me. People, the same people I had laughed and joked with only a few days before, avoided contact with me as they noticed the stark white bandages wrapped around both my wrists. No doubt I was emitting some heavy fuck-off vibes. Previously on the ward, I had reverted into the friendly, funny, 'hail fellow, well met' character that I had refined over the years but now they were seeing behind the mask into the damaged eyes of the real me. Nobody was laughing now.

On that first day back, the staff allowed me to rest for much of the time as I slept off the effects of the previous night but as soon as I woke, I was escorted (I was back on the close-observation regime) through the labyrinth of corridors in the late evening for an interview with one of the hospital's senior psychiatric consultants. Up until then, I had only been seen by psychiatric nurses or, on occasion, a first-year duty psychiatrist, so this was to be a consultation with the unknown.

I sat down in the small, compact consulting room opposite a

dapper white-haired gentleman in his early 50s with a flamboyant handlebar moustache. He wore a charcoal-grey three-piece suit with a light-blue shirt, finished off with a hand-tied pink bowtie. His deep, educated, accentless brogue soon dispelled any notion I might have been entertaining of him being a bit of a wacky eccentric, as he spoke knowledgeably and with authority about my case. I was impressed – and a little intimidated. He was completely objective and non-judgemental, and although I was still a bit woozy from the drugs, I found it easy to confide my inner fears. My self-loathing and all the baggage that came with it were poured out to that man that night. He said that a closer eye would be kept on me and I would attend daily one-to-one counselling sessions with him or his registrar until I was deemed trustworthy and rehabilitated enough not to try to hurt myself again.

His treatment plan had me improving in no time, as I responded well in the sure knowledge that I was in a place of safety. I was still being prescribed anti-depressants and painkillers but I had stopped for the time being with the sleeping pills. After being on the ward for a full week, I had my close-obs status removed. It felt like a minor triumph. I could again come and go as I pleased, knowing that I could return to the security of the hospital whenever I chose, under a 9 p.m. curfew.

I even returned to my part-time job. Being an in-patient in a psychiatric hospital on the one hand, while maintaining a relatively normal façade to the outside world, was a surreal experience. Only my immediate supervisor knew about my troubles and was satisfied that I could function well enough to perform my hardly challenging duties so long as I wore long sleeves to cover the dressings on my wrists. It was important that I turned up, as my absence could have had serious implications for me. Officially, I was earning only £15 per shift, with one or two shifts per fortnight. Unofficially, I was part of a scam (a scam that I still can't go into detail about) that saw me taking away £150 to £350 per shift. The scam had started as a way to make 'beer money' and, although I was still in the learning phase, I recognised the massive long-term potential of what was such a low-risk crime.

The part-time job was just an easy way for me to make an undeducted full-time wage and as I was unable to work for more than a few hours at a time due to the combination of my physical disability and fragile emotional health, it suited me just fine. But, as ever, later on there would be a price to pay. There was never any moral dilemma for me, as the scam involved removing a small percentage of the day's takings from a large commercial organisation, and as it grew, one of the biggest reasons I continued to do it was the feeling of getting one up on those who were ignorant about what I was up to. I was doing it, eventually, just because I could. Simply put, the larger the amount of money burning a hole in my back tail, the bigger the buzz. The biggest buzz I would ever experience was one to the tune of £4,800 for less than six hours' work.

It was far too easy and there were very few considerations to worry about. The only one of any import was the vital discipline of keeping my mouth shut. Although I was dealing with relatively small amounts at the time, I knew that one slack-jawed remark could very well result in a spell inside and while I was living with difficult-to-manage emotional issues, I wasn't totally stupid.

One thing that I remain grateful for during my stay in the Royal Ed was my visitors. My mum was a regular, Ross and his wife came up several times, but the one I appreciated the most, who came regularly and made me feel so much better, was the ever-loyal Rebekah. She would stroll into the ward, Daniel, now ten months old, staring around from the buggy. She brought me cigarettes and game cartridges for the console she had lent me and would happily sit chatting in the TV room as our son sat quietly lapping up the cooing of the other patients and staff. The best times during those visits were when the three of us, weather permitting, would take a leisurely wander through the hospital grounds. I never told Rebekah just how important those visits were, particularly the times the three of us were alone together. It was, in the most unlikely of circumstances, the first time I felt like an integral part of a real family unit. There we were, in this incongruous setting, meandering through large gardens criss-crossed with pathways, doing what for most people would be the most normal thing in the world, and I would be bubbling under with, for once, positive emotions.

I felt elated that Rebekah hadn't turned her back on me when most others had, even though she had more reason to than most. I was slowly beginning to fall in love with her but felt unable to show it or even say it. As I neared my discharge date, with her encouraging me and gently cajoling me, I began to see glimmers of hope and glimpses of a future.

29

Surfacing

MAY 1994

One day in May 1994, Rebekah collected me from the Royal Edinburgh Hospital and delivered me safely to my mum's. Mum had agreed to let me come back and both of us would make a monumental effort to get along with each other.

I started to spend more time with Rebekah and Daniel, and after a few weeks I was invited to stay at Rebekah's when her parents went on holiday. Although I still harboured a bit of resentment towards the toddler who was my son, as I spent more time with him I did naturally warm to him. I was in a position where I had as much or as little contact as I wanted with Daniel, without having any of the practical responsibility.

I did enjoy this period, getting to know Rebekah as a person all over again, but our relationship remained purely platonic. I was in no position psychologically to enter a sexual relationship. It was, for the time being, a situation without pressure and that seemed to suit us both. Although I shared Rebekah's bed, there was no physical contact between us. There was that ever-present barrier of the pregnancy occurring after the first time we had ever had sex and that was something I would continue to struggle with for a long time to come.

Shortly after Rebekah's parents returned from holiday, we were asked to house-sit again, this time for her brother, who lived close to his parents. I had arranged to go out on a Friday night with my old mate Tony for a few drinks and we ended up in the pub in which I had first met Rebekah, where I still knew many of the regulars. I was a bit wary of facing so many old acquaintances, as I felt they would all judge me as a mental case, but even if that was the case, nobody appeared particularly bothered, greeting and treating me as if recent events hadn't occurred. It was a fairly normal, non-eventful evening until I left after last orders and headed towards the main road, where I would hopefully flag down a taxi.

As I walked along the backstreet, pleasantly pissed, a coldness came over me. I had stopped dead in my tracks right outside the building in which I had been raped seven years before. I was face to face with something that had been an unleashed memory, a vile memory, but only a memory, and there in the silence of the early hours of a mild Saturday morning it became tangible.

I cried.

I stood shaking and sobbing, alone and disorientated. I had to get away but didn't know where to go. In the end, I climbed into a taxi and headed south to Rebekah's brother's, where she lay sleeping, unaware that the demons were on the march yet again.

Initially, I sat on the edge of the bed in which Rebekah slept, just rocking back and forth, mumbling nonsense to nobody in particular. When she woke, I was sobbing uncontrollably and as she moved towards me to comfort me, I snapped. Stripped to the waist and now screaming hysterically, the combination of the alcohol and mania taking control, I went into the adjacent bathroom and sought out the thing that I needed to remove the evil from my soul.

I returned to the bedroom in a state of delirium and haphazardly set about criss-crossing a random bloody pattern on my chest and upper arms. I was hyperventilating as the skin broke all over my upper body and the blood crawled downwards, staining my jeans and trainers. I was a mess of bright, angry, bleeding red lines but even witnessing something as shocking as this Rebekah remained composed and held

153

me close to her until, my energy spent, I calmed down. She put my shirt back on me and lay me down on the bed, slowly soothing me with her words until I fell into a fitful sleep.

Where most people would have succumbed to the fear that Rebekah must have felt, she dealt with the tantrum with kindness. She tried to nurse the madness out of me. Love on that level doesn't come along very often and yet I remained unable to accept it. The horror of what she had witnessed made her care more for me. As much as I needed to be loved, I also needed *to* love. I was in love with her but the fatal mistake I made was that I never said so. We did talk, and I was receiving some out-patient support from the Royal Edinburgh Hospital, but I needed so much more than that.

After returning from my part-time job one Saturday evening, I put it to Rebekah, with whom I was now living, that I would like to introduce her and our son to my father. With a few quid in my tail, we literally, there and then, got into her car and headed through the night to visit my dad. While I never said as much at the time, I wanted to show them off to my dad. I was proud that they were a stable part of my life and that I had, with their help, managed to bounce back. A part of me also wanted to rub his nose in it a wee bit and show him that I was a far better, more loving, conscientious father than he had been or could ever hope to be. Added to that was the fact that I had last spent time with him a week before I jumped from the window and so he hadn't seen me since I became a cripple. I still had many unresolved issues that I needed to speak to him about and, while they would remain unresolved, it was with a sense of false optimism that I travelled through that late summer night with my family.

Unsure of what to expect at my father's, not even certain he was still living at the address where I had last visited him, we felt it wise to book into the grubbiest guest house in the whole of the Western world, where we slept for a few hours before driving the remaining miles to his address. As it turned out, it was just as well we had booked in somewhere, because as we drove into the cul-de-sac where he lived I recognised with much surprise the house guest who had obviously had the same idea. The coincidence in our timing was a shock to us both and I was staggered to recognise my sister coming out of Ray's front door and removing something from the boot of her car. Talk about a fluke, but they do say that blood is thicker than water. My sister and I had grown apart and hadn't maintained any regular contact for a good few years, and it was with more than a hint of surrealism that we stood facing each other, just yards apart, hundreds of miles away from our home city, on the driveway of our absent, estranged father's domain.

Ray appeared glad to see us but I could tell he was less than comfortable being confronted in the flesh by both his abandoned children at the same time, both complete with partners and kids. Ray being Ray, though, he blustered and charmed his way through the afternoon and into the early evening.

Once again, my dad had remarried, this time to the stout, ginger-haired Irish woman I had met on my last visit, who was also the mother of my three-year-old half-sister. I was quite taken aback when I learned that my new 'step-mum' was a few months younger than me, consoled only by the fact she was an equal amount of stones heavier. Looking at his new family, I cynically wondered how long it would be before he upped sticks and fucked off, leaving them in the lurch and placing this new child in the same position of vulnerability as he had his first set of kids 23 years previously.

As night fell on that Sunday, I was only too glad to return to Hotel Scabby and would have been happy to head back up the road the following day had we not been invited back round to Ray's. It would have been rude to refuse such a magnanimous invitation after all he had done.

The thing is, in truth, something driving me inside made me stay. I was hoping against hope that my father and I could have a healthy relationship of sorts. I still wanted my dad. I still needed my dad. The child within craved the love of his daddy so much it carved him up into a million little pieces inside, but the adult I was knew that it was only a matter of time before my father and I would reach new heights of estrangement and have no contact ever again. The child within still clung to the hope that his dad would compensate him for the lifetime

155

of forgotten Christmases and birthdays (39 of each so far now and counting), he wanted the closeness only a father can provide but which had been denied him, he needed to love his dad and for his dad to love him back (or should it be the other way around?), but the adult I was knew, intellectually, that it had been an impossible quest. My 'Dad'-shaped void, I realised, would never be filled.

The following day, the Monday, proved the adult I was correct, as it was indeed the last-ever time I spent with my father. I could see in glorious, mind-numbing Technicolor that he had his new life and it was made fairly clear that I was superfluous to requirements. I was not to be a welcome part of my father's new family. Although we exchanged pleasantries that day, there was an undertone of mutually felt finality about it.

Immediately prior to our departure, he did something so normal, so simple yet so painful that it sent shards of anguish through every minute part of me. I did not show anything on the outside but inwardly I was devastated. In the space of a minute or so, I died a hundred agonising deaths. Not wanting to create a scene, I kept quiet but when he sat my half-sister on his knee, playing with her, bouncing her up and down in that frivolous yet protective way only dads can, then reading her a story from a kiddies' picture book, inside I was screaming frantically: 'IT SHOULD HAVE BEEN ME. WHY NOT ME? YOU'RE MY DAD, TOO, I'M YOUR FUCKING FIRSTBORN, YOUR ONLY SON. WHY NOT ME, YOU FUCKING EVIL, TWISTED, FUCKED-UP CUNT OF A DAD?' I was angry and I hated him. I hated this shitty world and all that was in it. I hated.

As usual when around him, I said nothing as I stood watching in resentful, jealous agony. Nothing except 'Goodbye, Ray.'

I've had no contact with him since.

It wasn't long before I slipped back into abusing sleeping tablets. I'd stay up all night in an unsteady stupor, fighting the drug and enjoying its weird effects. Rebekah at no time protested or hassled me as my sleeping pattern became ridiculous but she must have become frustrated at being left on her own with Daniel for long periods throughout the day. We quickly drifted into the first of many cycles of living separate lives, with me emerging bleary-eyed from my daze later and later in the day until eventually I was getting up when Rebekah was going to bed and vice versa. As my drug abuse accelerated out of control, I had no idea that I could do myself any physical damage with those innocent sleeping pills. Naively, I assumed them to be fairly harmless if they could be freely obtained without prescription, so I took larger and larger quantities in accordance with my ever-increasing tolerance. Also around this time, my legs had started to deteriorate and I had been prescribed reasonably high doses of an opiate-based compound. As ever, I exceeded the stated dose.

One morning, after lying on the sofa watching TV all through the night yet again, I stood up and felt a sharp pain in my lower back. Despite the huge amounts of drugs inside me, I realised there must be a problem but even after seeing blood instead of urine when I went to the toilet, I said nothing to Rebekah. I would sleep it off. I decided I'd try to detox for a couple of days and go to hospital if the pain and bloody urine persisted.

As it was, the pain got worse and I was admitted to hospital with nephritis, a kidney problem. Nothing particularly bad was coming back from blood tests, as I was taking the drugs legitimately, and the doctors never really asked any tricky questions. So, as always, I hid my drug misuse but I knew within myself that was what had caused the problem and so it was with much surprise and no little delight on my part that I was given an intravenous shot of morphine for the pain. I knew that it was the large, regular overdoses of diphenhydramine that had damaged my insides and so I resolved never to use such large amounts regularly. I didn't decide to stop abusing the drug absolutely, just not as often. I was kept in hospital for five days after a scan had shown that a portion of one of my kidneys had eroded away. After I was stabilised over the week, I was sent on my merry way with the obligatory blue plastic bag full of all sorts of drugs, including a codeine-based analgesic and a new drug prescribed to assist the kidney to return to full function. This drug was called Nefopam, and what a night lay ahead of me with that little box of tricks.

157

Rebekah came to pick me up and on the way home we stopped off at a shopping centre, where she bought me the latest console game to cheer me up. It was a cold, damp, miserable night and I was looking forward to sitting in front of the telly, playing my new game and munching my way through the contents of the blue polythene bag without giving a second thought to spending time with my girlfriend (who had visited me every day) or Daniel. Frankly, I couldn't wait for her to go to bed so that I could burst open my bag.

Later that night, safe in the knowledge both Rebekah and Daniel were asleep, I made a start. I lay on the sofa and took what I considered to be a safe amount of the new drugs. I lay back, eyes on the flickering TV, waiting for the pills to wave their magic wand. While the effects of the codeine were familiar to me – they always brought a feeling of warmth and laid-back contentment – the Nefopam was a completely new ball game.

As I lay back, basking in the flickering glow from the telly, I lost track of all time. I soon realised something different was happening to me. I had never experienced hallucinatory effects before. I was overcome with an inexplicable, unreasonable, bone-chilling sensation of fear as, first, Rebekah's small rubber plant that lived on top of the telly started moving towards me whispering murderous threats. The plant was telling me in a sinister, horror-movie voice that it was going to strangle the life out of me and, although I knew it was the drugs, it appeared only too real.

I squirmed, curling up into as tight a ball as I could manage against the armrest of the sofa, whimpering like a child. I discovered by accident that I only had to look away and the plant would sneak back into its pot but on the second occasion I did this, averting my eyes to the far end of the room, the wallpaper had come alive with thousands of mice – creatures that, along with rats, truly terrify me. The mice were running up and up but never came down, there was just a writhing carpet of filthy brown fur, black shiny eyes and vile smooth pink tails wriggling upwards but never down, ascending into nothingness as more and more took their place.

Next, from the opposite side of the room, I heard, really heard, a loud, angry, animalistic roar. I turned away from watching the rodents and saw, where only minutes before our recently acquired brindle boxer dog Basil had been sleeping peacefully, a full-sized orange and black tiger looking directly at me, its mouth hanging open to reveal huge razor-sharp teeth dripping with blood.

I have no recollection of the hallucinations ending but a mixture of raw fear and the chemicals in my body must have knocked me out, as the next thing I remember clearly is feeling a bright light penetrate my closed eyelids through the uncovered windows. Daytime had never been so welcome.

Breathing a huge sigh of relief, I peeled myself from the sweat-stained cushions, gathered up the remaining drugs and took them through to the bathroom. It was the only time I flushed any drugs down the toilet but the previous night had been too much to take. Never again. I crawled into bed beside Rebekah, holding her close to me for all I was worth.

30

Family Man

1995–96

My legs continued to deteriorate and with the threat of amputation looming large again, Rebekah paid for a holiday for the three of us in Corfu two months before I was due to return to hospital for an operation.

Away from the constraints of home life, I really began to appreciate her all over again. While we still did our own thing, we also spent a fair bit of time together. Since my encounter with the tiger, mice and homicidal houseplant, it was with a clear head that I saw the loving family I had in my grasp.

Things between Rebekah and myself were pretty good but there were still problems with our 'separate' lives, which meant that certain aspects of our togetherness remained, at best, sporadic. Even when I did feel sexually drawn to her (which was more often than I would ever demonstrate), I often found it hard to make any move. The sexual tension built up until the very last night of the holiday, when I returned from a local bar full of Dutch courage. As we were together under the stars, I couldn't help but wonder why it couldn't be like that at home.

That night something wonderful happened – not only did my heart finally let Rebekah in but we added to our family. When the pregnancy was confirmed, I was genuinely happy. I had learned a great deal from the mistakes I had made since the conception of Daniel. This new baby would reap the benefits and would seal the relationship between his parents hopefully once and for all. He had been conceived at a time when we had grown closer than we had ever been before and I hoped that that in itself would surely mean he would be born into a better environment.

After the operation, we decided to move from Edinburgh to a town in the Scottish Borders, where we would have a bigger house. Pregnant Rebekah took charge of everything as I was once again in plaster and on crutches. Although we were back to living almost separate lives – me by night and Rebekah by day – it was by far the most settled I'd ever been in my life. Unfortunately, it wasn't to last.

Because of the increasing problems with my legs, I'd had to give up my part-time job and so we were living on the basic income of benefits. Things were a lot tighter now there was no longer a few hundred quid extra coming in whenever I worked but Rebekah coped remarkably and I selfishly let her get on with it. The only thing that I had to worry me was that after a brief interlude we once again slipped back into 'separate lives' mode, although it was my deluded, fractured ego which would put that down to Rebekah's lack of interest and ignore the fact that I was a useless, fat bastard who contributed nothing.

The situation was exacerbated when we moved into that detached cottage in the Borders town. I slept downstairs because of my mobility problems and Rebekah was upstairs with Daniel. Because of the situation with my health, I began to see Rebekah as the best that I was ever going to get, in a derogatory way. I was denying how I really felt. I loved her.

The operation I had undergone just before we moved southwards had not been as successful as I'd hoped. My options were fast running out and it was decided to attempt a new, experimental procedure under a new consultant. In the meantime, I would continue hobbling around on a leg that was in constant agony and looked like a huge, angry, swollen stump. As the pain had intensified, so had the strength and

161

dosage of the opiate-based painkillers I was being prescribed – and so I resumed my on–off secret love affair with drugs.

At that time, while I'd developed a significant tolerance to opiates, I never felt I was in any danger of developing dependence. I was happy to indulge in slight overdoses that controlled my pain and gave me some mild euphoria. I was careful to act as normally as possible, so nobody, not even Rebekah, would notice that I was always, ever so slightly, out of my face.

By the time the baby's birth was imminent, it was apparent that incomers to an insular town in such a rural setting were far from welcome. Rebekah in particular had been the victim of small-minded small-town hostility on more than one occasion. She was feeling increasingly isolated and disaffected, and before long she started driving up to Edinburgh every day to her parents purely for some company.

As spring arrived, Rebekah's belly had swollen to space-hopper proportions and in March 1996, we made the journey, together for once, to Edinburgh's Simpson Maternity Pavilion, where Daniel had been born.

On arrival, Rebekah was examined and initially told to return home but she was exhausted with the pregnancy and in significant pain, so eventually, reluctantly, they admitted her to the delivery suite. The staff said nothing would occur overnight and I was told to return fresh the next day, when Rebekah would be prepared for a C-section in the early morning. After a good night's sleep, I returned to Simpson's and witnessed an event I was totally unprepared for. For once, it was love, not demons, on the march.

31

Kearan

19 March 1996

The room is familiar. I feel like I've been in this room before. The stark, white, blinding overhead lights exaggerate every blemish and every flaw of the green-clad people busying themselves with the preparations required for the smooth execution of what will follow.

I'm clad in one of the green cotton space suits, too, excited anticipation passing from Rebekah's hand to mine and back again as we wait for the main event. Three years before, in these same circumstances I felt fear. Today, right here, right now, there is no fear. Rebekah is exhausted but not scared. She knows what to expect and she can cope.

I look at her and see love in her weary eyes. I hope the unspoken message from my own eyes conveys what I feel. I am grateful for her determination. Her unassuming persistence has paid off as I sit here, her hand in mine, with not a hint of discomfort.

She is the one.

I know now that she is my angel. Of that there is nothing surer and when this is all over I will make the request that will mean so much to her. Even angels need to feel wanted and loved.

Something is happening; there are voices. The voices are controlled yet urgent and I know that something is amiss. We think that we are old hands at this but in reality twice in three years hardly counts as a lifetime of experience. With my right hand holding hers and my left shaking as it struggles to hold a video camera over her left shoulder, the urgency turns to mild animated panic. The people in green are working frantically until a very small, still, silent wad of gore is procured from the re-opened wound in its mother's belly. The bundle is not placed on her breast as before; instead, words we don't hear are said to us and I follow the green-clad female who clutches the newborn into a nearby smaller room.

Rebekah is lying on her platform, once again sedated but not enough to mask the look of abandonment in the darkened hollows of her eyes. I race behind the green-clad woman as best I can on very nearly steady legs and stand in the room, which is empty save for a stainless-steel sink and a small elevated Perspex box. I say nothing but, as before, I am now scared. This is a different fear from the last time. I see my new son properly for the first time but with his eyes tightly shut he doesn't move and he makes no sound. I see that he is the colour of a summer sunset as the woman rubs him vigorously, staining the white towel with streaks of liquid rust. As she rubs harder, my son moves independently, involuntarily, just a twitch in one of his tiny arms but movement nonetheless.

And then . . .

And then a sound.

A sound that in a previous incarnation has irritated and enraged me to the point of despair. But not today. Today it is a sound that dispels despair.

Now I'm understanding. I understand fully what is meant by the word beautiful. Never before has a newborn, not even my own firstborn, been beautiful to me. But in this moment, the sanctity of life and its pure beauty is clear. Never before have I shed a tear of joy and as I look at the tiny fragile creature squirming before me in the Perspex box, I understand now the nature of joy. I understand the mistakes I have made so far in my life. I understand the needs of the creature's older sibling and as I reflect upon the many ways in which I have erred with him, for a fleeting moment I am sorry.

I feel as if my development is complete. My parental instincts have finally been unleashed. I stand unmoving, for how long I don't know, spellbound as I concentrate on my son's open mouth, his lower lip trembling as he exposes toothless gums. No teeth, no hair and poor eyesight; I love him beyond all rapture. He is his grumpy dad's grumpy wee man and he is the best thing ever to have happened to me.

The green woman wraps this most precious of treasures in soft white wool and places him into my arms. I take him carefully yet greedily and something unquantifiable flows from him to me. As I hold this fragile creature, his crying and trembling instantly cease and for the moment, this timeless moment, there is only him and me alone in the whole wide world. We are alone and nothing else matters. The manner in which his widening indigo eyes burn into my soul confirms what I have suspected from the moment I set my own eyes upon him. I know that I will love and protect this small creature for ever. He will reap the benefit of the lessons I have learned from his brother.

I am taking my son towards his mother. My badly deteriorating legs scream in agony but there are matters of more importance just now. Before I sit back down at her right-hand side, I softly place my priceless cargo into her arms. Behind the mask, she smiles, little knowing that I have just discarded my own mask. As she looks adoringly at her new son, I whisper honestly into both their ears, 'I love you.' And I mean it. I do love them. And this time I do not resent the love that I feel. I love and I am loved and I want to feel like this for ever.

After leaving the hospital, I shuffle painfully through the streets. Although my crippled body toils to take me on the long journey home, I reflect that there is something unusual in the way I feel today. My physicality, which is in dire need of repair, is urging me to topple but my mind takes the strain. I am not doing what my body insists I must: I am not falling and love isn't hurting.

32

Lawful and Wedded

1996–97

I'd become a father once again but the feelings on this occasion were so very different to the previous time. I realised that I should have felt the same way the first time around but the simple fact was I didn't. My second son would be the child that I connected with straight away, the person who taught me the meaning of the word 'bonding'. Thankfully, in time, I would become much, much closer to Daniel, but it would take a while. Kearan was never to provoke feelings of anxiety or anger in me, even as a baby. That day, one of my best friends was born.

It was the best day of my life.

Throughout the time we had lived together, Rebekah had often half-jokingly talked about getting married. She always approached the matter in a light-hearted manner but I knew she was serious. In the direct aftermath of Kearan's birth, there was nothing that the real me wanted more.

I'd longed for the security and the loving togetherness of marriage all my life. To feel I belonged had always been my fantasy after being conditioned as the 'outsider' for so long, When I looked at Rebekah as she slept, I saw a woman who loved me regardless of my many failings, a person who knew me better than I knew myself.

Lawful and Wedded

When we went to register Kearan's birth, I surreptitiously pocketed some marriage application forms. My ham-fisted way of proposing, later on that night when the kids were in bed, was to casually hand her the forms and a pen. Like a cocky simpleton with an air of 'whatever' about me, I uttered something like, 'Well, d'you fancy it?' And with that, one of the crappiest proposals ever, we were officially engaged.

We chose a date six weeks away, two weeks after the date I had been given for my next operation, the urgent one. When we submitted the forms, Rebekah had never looked happier.

With our youngest son entering his second month, I was, once again, admitted to hospital. The operation I was due to have involved, amongst other things, removing part of my left hip and using it to reinforce the deteriorated bone in my right ankle. I was prepared for yet more long-term incapacitation and excruciating pain but this time was a wee bit different. In terms of keeping my right leg attached to me, this was really the last-chance saloon and so I resolved to do everything I was told by my new medical team, no matter how irritating or uncomfortable.

Two days after the operation, I was told by the nursing staff that I could go home if I could walk down the length of the ward on my crutches. Every shuddering one-legged step required gritted teeth and resulted in a curtain of sweat (my weight had now ballooned to over 19 stone), but I eventually completed the lap required for my release. As I left the ward, I did something that would have been inconceivable to me only a matter of less than a year ago. With Rebekah patiently walking at my painfully slow pace on the way to her car, I basked in the attention my new baby received from patients and staff alike as he slept in his car seat.

I was in a right state physically. I couldn't stand, sit or lie down for any length of time with any degree of comfort no matter how many tablets I took. I was meant to be on strict bed rest, moving only when unavoidable – I was even to piss in a bottle – but the pain was unbearable and that first night out of hospital it seemed to me that there was no way I would be able to attend my wedding, which was only 16 days away.

On 8 May 1996, finances and circumstances dictated a modest day. Neither of us had told anyone of our plans except the couple we had asked to be witnesses to our legal union. In the lowest of low-key affairs, which would come to epitomise our married life, we tied the knot in a registry office. Rebekah looked stunning in a knee-length cream-coloured dress and matching frock coat with nearly-white stockings and elegant high-heeled cream shoes. I looked like the big, fat, crippled bastard I was with my black plaster cast (coloured to match my suit) and the obligatory steel crutches that flanked my ample trunk. The service itself was fairly quick and efficient, and even with the time involved in taking photos, signing the register and the like, we were in and out in less than half an hour, but crucially, and potentially extremely dangerously for me, I was upright for all of that time.

I'd defied the strict instructions that had been imposed on me by my medical team, who had said that I had to remain on my back with my legs elevated for a minimum of six weeks. I knew better, of course, and I didn't think the odd half hour here or there would do much damage, even though I was struggling on the morning of the wedding. I had let Rebekah down far too many times before that day and would have moved mountains not to revert back to selfish behaviour on what was her special day. She told me as we left the registry office that she couldn't actually believe that I had gone through with it, having expected me to change my mind the minute I opened my eyes that morning.

After the simple service, we went for an equally simple meal in a quiet pub/restaurant, where Rebekah got changed out of her wedding clothes and popped across the road to break the news to her parents. At the same time, I called my mum from the payphone at the door of the pub, informing her that she had entered mother-in-law territory. She was pleased. Rebekah's parents agreed to keep the boys overnight, so, with our witnesses, we drove the 25 miles south to our house, where I would playfully refer to her as 'Mrs Randall' while we posed for pictures with the Bollinger that had been on ice since the day we had bought our Argos wedding rings and respective outfits. The whole kit and caboodle had cost less than £500 – and Rebekah had paid for everything.

It was not the sex that was to be the most memorable part of our first night of married life. At around four in the morning, I was awoken by a severe pain in my bad leg. As I investigated further, I saw that the toes peeking out of the plaster had swollen to the point where they looked like a row of over-ripe cherry tomatoes. Blood was seeping through the front of the cast, staining the bed sheets. Even after swallowing a few more painkillers than I should have, the pain was nowhere near to abating. After a phone call and a quick dash back up the road, my first full day of being a husband was spent in hospital.

As a result of being upright for far too long the previous day, the area around the operation site had swelled until it had become restricted by the cast, which caused the still-stapled wound to burst open and bleed to release pressure.

On admission, my cast was removed and I looked at what could easily have been confused with an elephant's leg, right down to the discolouration of the skin. Almost immediately on the removal of the cast, the swelling deflated, the pain evaporated and the pigment returned to the surface, and I knew I had been extremely lucky.

I was put on strict bed rest for 24 hours without a cast and when my leg had returned to its regular shape and size, the wound was fastidiously sterilised and re-stapled.

When I got home, Rebekah ran the household with efficiency. Although I was spending more time with the boys, particularly the younger one, my capabilities were limited. If I wasn't lying in my bed with the baby at my side watching telly, I was hobbling around on crutches, getting in the way more than anything else. Although she already had plenty of things to occupy her time, Rebekah also nursed me pretty much back to full health.

Some old habits refused to die and I'd slipped back into abusing my prescription drugs. As I was still able to stop and start abusing the medication as I wanted, I failed to realise that I was by that time in the early stages of developing an addiction, using the drugs for their secondary, euphoric, sedative effect and not the primary analgesic purpose for which they had been prescribed. They had become my means of escape, an easy way to alleviate the monotonous regularity of the four walls that had become my prison. At least with my drugs I could temporarily liberate my body and completely free my mind.

Five months after the operation, I was finally given a clean bill of health and it was clear that the new consultant had performed a minor miracle. The whole process had been a spectacular success, as I was able to walk unaided with very little pain and not the slightest suggestion of a limp. It was like being reborn and I started to live all over again.

Now that I was able to go back to work, we had an extra few hundred pounds of disposable income from the resumed scam job to play with and our standard of living improved. The cash was used to buy things for the kids and house. We ate better food, had no problems with bills and always had a few quid left over to spend on new clothes and books, videos or computer games. As my illicit income was regular, although unpredictable – usually ranging between £100 and £500 per shift – we also began to plan for the future in small ways. I was only too aware that the money could dry up at any time because of the criminality involved in obtaining it but this also presented me with a practical problem with saving. I was paranoid about banking the cash, so it was always spent as quickly as I'd stolen it.

Christmas that year was the first really materialistic festive season I had enjoyed and I would try from that time on to supersede the previous year's efforts until the festive season became insane. Christmas dinner was an event in itself, with me doing the cooking for what must have seemed to be a huge gathering even though there were only four of us to feed. The kids were provided with enough presents that year to have stocked a small toy shop but the looks on their faces was all that mattered to me – even at such a young age Kearan seemed to have some idea of what was going on, or maybe he was just bemused by the whole business. It was important that Christmas was a magical time and it was important for me to be the one in control of the magic wand.

The money I acquired gave me a sense of power that no doubt became a major factor in my long-term moral corruption and 1996 was just the beginning. On the face of it, I was happy but, underneath, all I was doing was financially over-compensating for my emotional failings.

Lawful and Wedded

In the New Year, Rebekah's homesickness got the better of her and we agreed to return to Edinburgh, so she organised a move into a three-bedroom house in the east of the city. All the rooms in the new house were small but it was a large property on three levels, including a floored attic.

I had, against all the predictions of my medical team, passed my driving test and filled Rebekah's car with small items to deliver to the new house. When I entered the place for the first time, I was horrified by the state of it and its noisy, busy location.

I hadn't realised just how much of a slob I had become until I had to put my back into lifting the heavier house contents into the hired van Rebekah drove for the removal. At almost 20 stone, I shouldn't have been surprised. I was in all sorts of trouble. I had really let myself go: sitting up alone through the night for month after month, shovelling all manner of comfort food down my wobbly neck quite relentlessly, only leaving my mouth empty long enough to suck on too many fags. The more I ate, the better I felt, and the bigger I got, the less I cared. The fact was that in another way I was destroying myself.

As the dynamic changed radically in my part-time job, resulting in a 14-week idle period, I set about making severe changes to my appearance. My overeating stopped as my intake went down to one low-calorie, no-fat meal a day, supplemented by snacking on fresh vegetables and drinking loads of water, with the odd cup of tea or coffee when I felt tired. In all, I was taking in less than 500 calories a day. Every night, I took the dog on a very steep walk up Salisbury Crags. Night after night I climbed; day after day I starved – and in the space of four months, I lost a shade under six stone.

Throughout the time I was dieting, Rebekah encouraged and motivated me. I wallowed in her compliments but was far too self-absorbed to realise she wasn't just saying it for its own sake but really meant it. Her sincerity was lost on me, as I only cared about myself and how quickly I was changing, and as time went on I fell into the trap of believing that I was turning into God's gift.

Tactility is something I value greatly in a relationship, but something I have never been able to slip into easily. I had never had a relationship

171

where spontaneous displays of love, romance or tenderness were indulged in and my relationship with Rebekah was probably the worst it got. Rebekah was (and remains – even more so as she has aged) very pretty, but all too often I chose to see her as the short, fat, dumpy lassie I had impregnated three years previously. Yes, there were times when I gave in to what my eyes told me but there was an invisible barrier I just couldn't get over. I loved her but couldn't tell her. She was the person who was then, and ever would be, closest to me, and that would remain a constant even when things went wrong. I wasn't able to admit just what I had and even now I am still not sure why. She was easily the best friend I ever would have and a soulmate who was there for me long before the term became fashionable. A woman without whom I was lost in the desert and yet I could never actually tell her just what she meant to me because of my retarded, damaged emotions. I spent a lot of money on her but there was an impersonal aspect to that, as though I considered the actual spending to be gesture enough. It was a tragic conundrum – every time my wife showed signs of loving tactility, I would shy away from it, but on every occasion I did so I knew it was what I needed and wanted from her more than anything else. I just couldn't accept her physical displays of love.

When, at the end of August, I returned to my part-time job, I was virtually unrecognisable from the fat, lazy bastard I had been only four months previously but I'd also fallen into 'fuckwit' mode at the same time.

The changes in the job offered an opportunity for a serious increase in criminal activity – whereas before it had been a case of working once or twice a fortnight, now there were opportunities to work up to four times a week. I was taking home thousands of pounds a week, while also receiving a wage from the job I was abusing and illegally claiming disability benefit. A friend had also offered me another job as a pub doorman, which I took, knowing it could validate my nocturnal lifestyle and widen my social circle.

I'd always been appalled by the behaviour of some of my married friends in the past when they were shagging around, so for me to even consider the prospect of extra-marital relationships was ludicrous. I was the last person in the world who would mess around and I was known for my attitude towards philandering. I have no idea why that attitude began to slowly and subtly change but the net result was dramatic. In the space of two years, I would go from being religiously monogamous to a disgraceful serial shagger. It is too easy for observers to say that I was unhappy. I know that I was not unhappy; I was the happiest and most secure I had ever been. My integral self-destructive mechanism subconsciously drove me, yet again, to create a situation that would ultimately come back and smack me between the eyes repeatedly.

As summer made way for the autumn of 1997, I was sexually unfaithful for the first time. A tall, large-framed, dark-haired female who also worked on the pub doors made obvious advances towards me as a group of us relaxed after a short weekday daytime shift. Abby had some kind of highly sexual allure. Eventually, as the day became night and we drank ourselves stupid, we headed back to her flat, where we had sex. Stupidly and almost immediately, I clouded the difference between love and sex and found myself developing feelings for her that didn't exist. Whatever the emotional implications of this act of betrayal were, I had broken my once-sacred golden rule of remaining faithful.

I was instantly liberated from any of my previous inhibitions regarding infidelity. I had crossed the line and I believed I could handle it. After all, most of my male contemporaries were shagging around, so why the hell shouldn't I? At least that's what I told myself. Married for just over a year, I embarked that night on a journey of dual identity – married with kids by day (when I was awake) and young, free and single by night.

When I arrived home the afternoon of the morning I had first been unfaithful, Rebekah appeared unmoved by the fact that I had disappeared for 36 hours. I tried to act exactly as I would have if nothing untoward had occurred but I was very self-conscious. It wasn't until she nipped out in the car and I was left alone with our younger son that I gave in to the sea of emotion I was drowning in. With Kearan on my lap, staring curiously and intently into my eyes, I cried the way I was used to seeing him cry when inconsolable.

That really should have been the end of my career as a two-timing bastard. I was only too aware that I had done wrong and that sickening feeling should have been more than enough to stop me in my tracks immediately. But it wasn't.

I would tell myself that Rebekah was to blame but it was just an excuse. The fact was that sex had always been important to me, not just for its own sake but as an expression of love. It was something I recognised. I knew that Rebekah loved me but I had talked myself into believing I needed more.

I needed to feel secure but I'd also developed a lifelong attraction to danger. I *did* want to hold hands or walk with our arms around each other in public, I *did* want to go out properly with Rebekah in company as the couple we were but something insurmountable prevented me from doing so.

Again.

33

Kerry and the Crippled Loser

1997–2000

With the operation giving me a new lease of life, I'd been drug-free since our move back to Edinburgh. I was enjoying my jobs, meeting new people and indulging in a hectic social life. I was also spending more money, as my ill-gotten gains increased steadily.

In the early part of October 1997, I foolishly thought – like many others – that being drunk was no obstacle to driving home one night. Of course, I was caught. The two cops who stopped me were actually really decent and treated me well. I had been drinking heavily for almost ten hours but had sobered up very quickly, although I was well over the legal limit. I was formally charged and searched, eventually being fined a few hundred pounds and getting disqualified for 15 months. I'd done it again; I had nobody and nothing to blame but my own stupid self.

I began to go out even more at night. At weekends, I would finish working on my pub door around 1 a.m. and go to a nearby club. I believed that for as long as the money was rolling in, I could behave with impunity.

175

Christmas was, in terms of money spent, the best I had ever experienced. I saw it as a way to show those I loved just how much they meant to me in an accountable, quantifiable fashion. I bought new TVs, jewellery, gadgets, videos, CDs, clothes, games consoles, expensive cosmetics and more unnecessary toys for the kids. On the morning of the day Santa had done his stuff, the sitting room floor was invisible. I'd done my job. I felt a somebody in my own home. I genuinely cannot remember Christmas Day being special or outstanding in any way during my own childhood. But now it was perfect – on the surface.

The period between Christmas and New Year saw me working constantly at my two jobs. By day I was scamming hundreds of pounds and by night I had moved from my relatively quiet pub door in the Grassmarket to the more hectic environment of a newly renovated nightclub.

Hogmanay was absolutely heaving and so when the club closed its doors to the public, I volunteered to stay at the door on the inside to ensure no one gained entry when anyone chose to leave. I found myself sharing the landing with an attractive, tallish female in her early 20s. She had a strong-looking, athletic yet curved body crammed into a figure-hugging silk, short-skirted, oriental-style dress, with perfect legs encased in tight, black, knee-length boots. All this was underneath a precisely sculpted mop of long, dark-brown curls. She was effervescent and confident. She was way out of my league. Not seeing her as a potential conquest, I relaxed and chatted away with her as she waited for her pal who worked in the club. Eventually, she moved on to a party in the company of her friend. Little could I have known that in a matter of a few months that girl would come to dominate each and every one of my waking thoughts.

I had just had my first encounter with Kerry.

The early part of 1998 saw me work hard and play harder. I was rarely at home, out every night of the week and working each weekend. I was making more and more cash all the time and running out of ways to spend it; by now, my whole day was inverted.

One night in early March, I headed into town to a club where I met Kerry again. Initially, I paid very little attention and as the club filled up I found myself feeding a greedy slot machine. As I fished out more and more cash, I turned and saw Kerry beside me. Before long, we were kissing passionately, hands everywhere without inhibitions, suddenly invisible in a room full of people. When we stopped, I grabbed her hand and made for the stairs. As we walked, we talked openly and intimately – I would always talk too much to her while she would become gradually more closed. From the start, I felt – hoped – that she, like me, was searching for love. Real love. I was flattered by her attentions. There was no sex that night but the promise of it was tangible. I was already in too deep.

A couple of nights later, I went to the club where Kerry was now working behind the bar and we left together. She drove us to a remote spot and parked under a huge overhanging tree. This was the first time that I was unfaithful to Rebekah without the excuse of alcohol.

Within three weeks, the relationship escalated to a very intense level. When I wasn't working at the club, she would spend a few hours with me as I stood on the other pub doors I worked before she went to start her own shift at 10 p.m. When I finished at the back of 1 a.m., I would walk up to the club, have a pint while I waited for her to finish, then sit in her car for a while before she dropped me off at home in the early hours.

I was falling for Kerry as quickly as she appeared to be falling for me. We became, to all intents and purposes, a proper couple. Rebekah's accusations that I was having an affair came pretty quickly and accurately. I came clean and assured her that I would end the relationship with Kerry immediately.

I didn't.

I couldn't.

I knew that I couldn't choose between them. I didn't see it as 'having my cake and eating it', as I had a huge need and capacity to give and receive love. The love I'd craved all my life was finally coming in abundant quantities and I wouldn't give it up easily whatever price might have to be paid. In the space of 30 years, I'd come from having a heart devoid of all love to a place where I was positively brimming over with it. How I was going to keep a hold of all this love was a mystery.

The relationship with Kerry went on and the intensity of it stunned me. I found myself telling her things – after she questioned me – that I'd never thought I would ever reveal to another human being. I told her about my emotions, about my suicide attempts, about what I hoped for in my life. She listened to it all, absorbed every word, and before I knew it she had everything she would ever need to manipulate me should she choose to do so.

I recklessly pursued a hedonistic, cheating lifestyle, which was now, in mid-1998, no longer regarded as a secret. I was causing a great deal of hurt and pain to Rebekah but I believed the money I was throwing at my marriage would cushion the blow all round.

Throughout the summer, I spent every available minute with Kerry. I felt like a teenager. The situation became more normalised the longer it went on. Kerry became increasingly annoyed about my ongoing reluctance to leave Rebekah, but, as usual, I believed the money I was throwing around would sweeten the pill. I had been promoted in my part-time job and the rewards had increased. With my benefits, security job and part-time job, which I was using as a means to commit fraud, my average take-home income was often almost £3,000 a week. I had neatly folded bundles of £1,000 secreted throughout the house – in my golf bag, a small silver box that sat on the mantelpiece, the cabinet on my side of the bed – and a row of £1,000 wads sitting on top of books on a bookcase in the bedroom. I was making it quicker than I could spend it. Nights out with Kerry soon became overnight stays in Edinburgh's top hotels. Although my driving ban wouldn't be up until the early part of 1999, I had even bought a Jaguar sports car in preparation for that day.

Nothing changed over the next few months. I kept seeing Kerry, I kept living with Rebekah. It was repetitive, it was unsatisfactory, but I kept going with it as it had quickly turned into normality for me. I continued to buy the loyalty of the two women in my life.

Every day/night was pretty much the same – work to do and money to steal. I was just about able to get through but always returned home exhausted and emotionally ragged. The embezzlement I was involved in had also become normalised. In the past, I had experienced an exhilarating rush from my criminal activities but now I was working on auto-pilot more and more. On some nights, I only took the money out of a fear that neglecting to do so would compromise me. I had so much money that I thought throwing it around could solve every problem. I would attempt to buy myself happiness, love and loyalty for a long time yet to come.

At one point, Kerry and I went on holiday together – a major mistake. It was so clear from the start that we were wrong for each other. While on the surface we appeared to be complementary types, the fact is that we were too similar in vital ways. Perhaps in response to my behaviour, Kerry appeared needy, as if she was crying out to be loved. There seemed to be no end to it – I would decide that I needed to end things with her but then panic about how I would live without her; I thought Rebekah was all I wanted, then I slept with Kerry.

Christmas came around again and I spent money like there was no tomorrow, whereas tomorrow would actually just bring more scamming and more money I had to spend (in fact, on Boxing Day 1999, I ended up £2,500 better off). Every penny of my income at this point was illegal. I was still in receipt of benefits, which therefore rendered both my claim and indeed the wages I earned the proceeds of crime. Added to this were the now huge amounts of cash I was obtaining fraudulently through my part-time job. I only really needed the job to access the growing opportunities to make a lot of money. In the year ahead, with my fingers in a few more pies (or tills), I would end up taking home well over £100,000 in tax-free 'earnings', most of which I squandered or gave away to the two women who were a constant in my life, both seemingly accepting of my philandering ways.

Kerry had recently moved into a flat with my ostensible encouragement as I made countless empty promises of commitment to her. I had become a more devious and accomplished liar as my affair with Kerry had intensified and this sort of duplicity came easily to me as all I was doing was attempting to buy myself some guilt-free time with her. The pattern was forming without my realising it. There is only so long that you can split yourself in two before eventually tearing your whole self apart and that was what I was doing.

Could I handle it?

Of course I could.

As far as Kerry was concerned, although I had developed extremely strong feelings for her I always justified cheating on her to myself as I felt she knew the score. I felt a hell of a lot more guilt in terms of Rebekah and that, alongside my instinctive desire not to get caught, meant that the lies became second nature to me. I would often believe them myself and lie on many occasions solely for lying's sake. It was a bloody mess but I couldn't see what I was doing. I genuinely felt that I was in love with both women and as a consequence was unable to break away from either.

One day I received a text from Kerry asking that I phone her urgently. I took the dog out for a walk and as soon as I was out of view of the house I wearily dialled her number on my mobile. Kerry sounded nervous and made trivial small talk about nothing in particular. Picking up on her obvious reticence, I asked her what the matter was.

'I'm pregnant,' she said softly, her voice an apologetic whisper. Then silence. Given that I believed she was sterile, this time I had very good reason to ask the not-so-silly question, and 'How?' was all I could come up with as a comet of thoughts shot through my mind. This couldn't be happening. It must be a wind-up, a mistake, a way to pressure me to move out. Our relationship had been an affair without any serious consequences to contemplate and now I was faced with the most serious consequence of all. In the space of that five-minute phone call, my whole mindset and attitude towards her changed. This had certainly not been part of the plan. In no way, shape or form did I want any more kids, not with Kerry, not with Rebekah, not with anyone. But I believed I loved Kerry at this time and, trapped as I felt, I just couldn't make the break.

No matter what lies I told Rebekah, there would be no explaining this one away but I couldn't face telling her about the situation right then. She took the boys on holiday and I hated it – the house was heavy with the silence of the solitude I thought I craved and became little more than a bunker I had dug myself into as I chose to opt out from my life for the two weeks I would spend alone. It was as if a huge part of me had embarked on the same flight to Spain alongside my family. This was

180

the first time I had been physically alone since taking up with Rebekah properly in late 1994 and I was simply unable to cope without her and the boys. The fear I felt when having no choice but to live alone, to face myself on a constant basis, was practically insurmountable.

I had no escape from myself.

I went into several chemist shops dotted around the city and armed myself with enough sleeping pills to put myself in a position where the 14 days of loneliness could be served. In my more lucid moments through my self-induced fug, I missed Rebekah like crazy. It wasn't what she did for me, and that was a great deal, it was the person she was. She had become my rock but somehow, instead of actually telling her that, I violated her huge, altruistic heart. I took her for granted, assuming that no matter what I did, she would always be there for me, always love me. I had the love I'd so desperately strived to find right there in the palm of my hand and yet I expended little energy embracing it. My fucked-up inability to deal with this purest of pure love seemed to have no roots. Maybe I had just been born that way. The one thing that I wanted and needed so dearly was the same thing that I would reject until it was far too late.

When Rebekah returned, I still couldn't tell her how much I loved her. I also felt much less for Kerry when Rebekah was away. It was as if one of these women in my life had become insignificant unless set off against the permanency of the other. It was, as in every avenue of my life, all or nothing.

34

Bright, Shiny and New

2000—02

A new millennium, a new beginning, a new dawn.

Not for me.

Underneath the bluster and false confidence of my public persona, I was terrified of the future.

In mid-February, I was offered a job as manager with overall control of the door-stewarding operation with the security company and agreed to take it on for a trial period. The pressure of the job would be significantly intensified, as I now had sole responsibility for staffing around 40 separate licensed premises. As ever, I threw myself into my new role, initially glad of the distractions it offered me, giving 100 per cent commitment, but I soon learned that I was unable to do the job the way I felt it should be done. I felt I was being hampered in some way by my manager and rapidly became disillusioned, as it was increasingly obvious that I was being asked to fulfil a task while blindfolded with both hands tied behind my back.

I received a phone call on a Friday night as I was leaving Dundee, where there were three pubs to supervise. The call was from Kerry, phoning from hospital declaring that she had gone into labour and asking if I could get there as quickly as possible as the baby was well

182

on the way. I headed immediately for the hospital, arriving at just after 11 p.m. By this time, Rebekah was aware of Kerry's pregnancy and, although it was an unspoken spectre that haunted our life together, she seemed to accept and deal with it when I gave her assurances that, regardless of the new baby, I wouldn't leave her. The double life was becoming crazier as the complications, both physical and emotional, steadily increased.

Bewildered and disorientated, I hurriedly navigated the maze of corridors. Eventually, I found the appropriate labour suite. I entered the compact, clinical room, where I observed a very comfortable, nonchalant, calm Kerry, sitting up on a birthing bed, happily chatting away with her mother. I only have very sketchy recall of that night in March when I became a father to a little girl called Amy.

My relationships with both Rebekah and Kerry had levelled off. I was now in little more than a friendship with my wife and the intense passion of the affair with Kerry had gone. She knew that I had little real intention of ever leaving the marital home, despite her wish for me to get a divorce, and she moved out of Edinburgh. While I still found Kerry amazingly attractive and was firmly of the belief that I was very much in love with her, I was also able to recognise that in the instant she gave breath to another new life, the death knell of our stuttering relationship reverberated deafeningly and the flicker of illicit excitement echoed into the distance. We really should have called it a day there and then but, as similar people, we would string it out histrionically, me in particular, long after the sell-by date had expired.

That summer, I tried to spend more time at home with Rebekah and less with Kerry and Amy. I also went out with my pals more and more, as the situation with the new baby was a complication I just couldn't deal with. With money still rolling in easily, it created a psychological buffer zone for me – so long as I was chucking enough of it in Kerry's direction then active fatherhood would end there as far as I was concerned; I was simply buying freedom from responsibility. Rebekah and the boys were also being very well taken care of materially and I was paying for my own distorted version of the moral high ground.

The rest of the year went by in a predictable fashion – Kerry, Rebekah, arguments, theft, physical pain, drugs and the usual crazy Christmas had all been seen before and were all to be seen again. The spending in particular I found to be a catharsis, a way in which I could purge the perpetual nagging guilt and underlying deep-rooted feelings of unworthiness. As the money I spent increased with each passing year, my mum would castigate me for spoiling the kids but, as I retorted on every occasion, she would say that, wouldn't she? How could she understand that what I was really trying to do was recreate the childhood Christmases I never had? It gave me power and made me feel like somebody. That Christmas, for the first time, I was not just the king of the castle, I was the king of two castles. But even kings have a breaking point. Maybe on the surface I looked as if I had it all but, underneath, things were getting bad again.

By New Year, the old self-loathing had kicked in again and on returning to her house after a very drunken party at a friend's house, to which I had chosen to go with Kerry over Rebekah, I faced up to the reality that I was hurting too many people too often; every ounce of guilt, self-loathing and remorse I had ever felt flashed into my head. As Kerry lay naked beneath me, I looked straight into her black eyes and screamed psychotically, 'Fucking hit me, make me hurt, hurt me so much that I cry. Please, just fucking hit me.' The screaming pleas faded to defeated, flaccid sobs and eventually into a very disturbed sleep. The last thing I remember is a very scared expression on Kerry's face as she slid from underneath me and fled to a safer place that was somewhere away from me. The web of deceit I had been weaving started to take its toll and I slowly began to withdraw from my own life. On the outside, I was able to hide behind a veneer of normality but I knew I was slipping.

At this stage my relationship with the codeine-based drugs was one of greed as opposed to need. Yes, I required pain management but the normal dose was sufficient for me to function as normally as possible. On the days I didn't take them, I suffered no ill effects. The way in which I used the drugs was akin to the manner in which a weekend binge drinker abuses alcohol, an experience I was also well versed in. I had, again, grown accustomed to the pain in my legs but was using it as an excuse to overdose. My body hadn't yet grown accustomed to the chemicals that I would try to take away from it. I knew deep inside that I was cultivating dependence but I just couldn't care less. I believed that if the time came when I thought I was being compromised, then I'd just stop taking them.

By the tail end of 2001, my relationship with Kerry had, for various reasons, all but petered out and I had inwardly resolved to end it completely in the New Year – a resolution I was to keep for all of six weeks. It was time for another Hogmanay, another nothing shift at my other job and another New Year party at Ross's, where this time I had arranged to meet up with Rebekah and the boys when I had finished work. It was just after the bells – when I kissed my wife passionately and told her truthfully how much I loved and needed her and that I wanted nothing more than to make a real go of things with her from then on – that a faceless stranger from the previous year's party assumed Rebekah was Kerry and announced he was delighted to meet her. Again.

I slipped outside into the silence of Ross's driveway and sent a cold, distant, uncongenial, almost random text message to Kerry. 'Happy New Year' was all it said but I was well aware of the implicit subtext when I pushed the send button with my thumb, a subtext that was understood the moment the message was received.

With the party spirit knocked out of us, we gathered our children and decided to call it a night fairly early on. Very little was said between us as the boys collapsed in heaps on their beds but the relative silence that heralded our New Year – the first we had actually brought in together – spoke volumes.

Despite my intentions of concentrating on my legitimate family, I cracked after a self-imposed six-week ban on seeing Kerry and went round to visit her. We picked up where we had left off and the relationships with both women in my life became more and more fractious as I flitted between both houses, lying to both of them about my relationship with the other. Kerry in particular was pissed off by the fact that in the two years since Amy had been born, I had paid very little attention to her, avoiding any parental responsibilities by doing what I always did – throwing money around. No longer willing to tolerate my ways, Kerry now stung me permanently with a text comment. It wasn't the phrase 'deadbeat dad' that bothered me so much as what followed it: 'CRIPPLED LOSER'. The accuracy hit me more than the nastiness.

Despite the animosity between us, Kerry was still pressuring me to move out of Rebekah's and I was constantly lying to Rebekah. Obviously not very well, as one afternoon early in 2002 I returned to find her throwing black bin bags full of my clothes from the window of 'our' bedroom. At first, I stood helplessly beside my car, mesmerised by the bin bags plummeting towards me and exploding on the ground at my feet, spewing the clothing out. Not wanting to face up to the reality of what was happening, I laughed uncontrollably until my sides felt bruised with exertion. The tears were less than an hour away and through my loud guffaws I knew I was only putting off the inevitable. The monster I had been busy creating over the past four years had just taken its first tentative steps into the real world. My real world.

I threw the contents of the bags into the back of my car and sped off towards Kerry's house, first stopping off at a few shops to get my little white pellets of peace. Sitting on a metal bench inside the shopping mall without a care for who might see me, I quickly released 12 of the 24 tablets from their foil strip and swallowed them gratefully. Up until that point, I had never taken such a large amount of the drug in one go, and this was the first time I had consciously used it as a solution to a problem. I was very surprised at the intensity of the initial hit. Previously, the warm, safe sensation had crept up on me almost unawares but this time it smacked me full on as I drove at 80mph along the city bypass to Kerry. I allowed the warmth to encase me completely as the car seemed to guide itself automatically to her house. By taking all of those tablets at once, I had upped the stakes. As I ate more and more of the tablets over the coming months, I found that all the self-awareness in the world is no match for the hold of an addiction.

I arrived at Kerry's outwardly calm and told her that I had left Rebekah for good. I sat on the edge of the double bed in her bedroom, smoking absently while I listened to Amy and her half-sister happily playing outside in the garden, the sound of which drove home to me just how serious this situation actually was. I thought about my younger son and what I was doing to him. With the image of his open, innocent face clear in my mind, I broke down violently in front of Kerry, struggling to talk through my breathless sobs. Ever practical, she told me to go home, that this was not right and to, at the very least, talk to my son and try to explain to him what was happening – as if I knew myself. There was no way out.

I took Kerry's advice, got back into the car, swallowed the remaining 12 tablets and made the return journey in a daze. With my eyes stinging and red with too many tears, I stopped off at another late-opening chemist for more drugs before driving to what used to be home. Walking up the external stairs to the front door, I made the conscious decision not to use my keys and knocked just loudly enough on the front door. Less than three hours had elapsed since I'd driven away but it was still long enough for Rebekah to have made herself even stronger and to tell me that there was no way I was getting back in – at least, not permanently.

Rebekah's attitude did soften a bit over time but she wasn't in a completely forgiving mood. A friend gave me the chance to rent a flat of his in Gorgie, which afforded the opportunity for me to think and also to show both Rebekah and Kerry that I wasn't spending time with the other. I was financing three houses and didn't belong in any of them.

I had reverted to the vulnerable self I was at the time of my hospitalisation in the Royal Edinburgh almost eight years previously and was careering towards another emotional and psychological breakdown. I had lost sight of any perspective on my life. The pressure of my criminal activities was taking a huge amount out of me, as the whole thing had become almost a cottage industry providing an income people, not least of all myself, were relying upon. I wanted to stop but I couldn't. Mistakes were being made and I, as a figurehead, had to account for any discrepancies, often dealing with other people's fuck-ups by replacing the missing cash with some of the dough I had stolen. Nobody else involved actually seemed to realise the implications of what they were doing and left it to me to clear up their shit. The biggest problem was that to stop abruptly would mean the appearance of a huge cash anomaly that would be immediately investigated and so it would have to be manipulated slowly to a seemingly natural halt. In late 2002, my personal life was in tatters and my professional life was catching up.

It was after another argument with Kerry that the spectre of self-harm re-emerged. On a Saturday afternoon, I swallowed a handful of sleeping pills along with my now-daily dose of 24 painkillers. The combined overdose was not designed to kill me but to sedate me enough so that I wouldn't register the pain of the dressing-gown belt I had prepared to hang myself with. It was a half-hearted attempt, as I couldn't get the knot right, and even when I thought I had, the belt was unable to hold my bulk. I even tried pulling both ends of it as tight as I could round my neck with both hands as I sat disorientated, frustrated and weeping miserably. It was in that position but horizontally buckled and semi-conscious that I was discovered by Rebekah when she returned in the early evening. She had known that I was sliding back into the darkness and, as before, she tried her best to help; but this time I was in a far deeper and darker place than even she had known. It was decided between us that I really ought to seek immediate help and after a phone call and an ice-cold sobering shower I made my own way back to the Royal Edinburgh Hospital.

While the place had not changed in appearance one little bit, the philosophy and administration more than made up for the lack of aesthetic differences. I was, as before, interviewed by a duty psychiatrist but sent away and advised to see my GP on Monday morning. I had told the doctor everything through sobs and tears: the drugs, the affairs, the double life, the criminality, the failing attempts at keeping it all together on the surface and, of course, the terrifying return of the suicidal demons that I just couldn't shake off, even after all these years of trying. I described my self-loathing and self-destructive impulses in as much detail as I poured out my unworthiness as a human being but, no, I was not ill enough to be admitted. For all that doctor knew, I was walking out to try again. As it was, I was exhausted in every way and drove numbly through the dark, wet Edinburgh streets back to

Rebekah, who, if the truth be told, was not particularly overjoyed to see my sorry arse back in her house. At this point, I was just over two months away from the final attempt I would make at putting an end to my fucked-up, never-ending, agonising existence.

Nothing really changed in those two intervening months as I functioned as well as possible in a trance-like state. If anyone apart from Rebekah or Kerry noticed something was amiss, they never mentioned anything to my face.

By the beginning of December, I had been told by Kerry that she was ending our fragile relationship. Although what was left of the pragmatist in me knew that this was the correct course of action, the ever needy emotional cripple found it so difficult to let go. I wrote her letters, sent her cards and put tokens of affection through her letterbox in the middle of many nights. I drove to her street and sat crying in my car often until daybreak. I had lost all sense of reality and it would be a hell of a long time before I would reclaim it, if, indeed, I ever did. I had become convinced she was playing mind games and in the process found myself out of my depth, losing my own mind.

My next attempt to kill myself properly, once and for all, was put into motion with almost militaristic planning a fortnight before I would actually attempt it. This was to be no impulse open to error. I would prepare for every eventuality and, as I did so, my mind travelled back to my days as a young boy. Almost since birth I had been in conflict with those close to me, especially my mother. In the intervening years, nothing much had changed. My mum had been left holding the babies and while I now acknowledge she did her best, she herself had been psychologically ill-equipped for the daily rigours of parenthood. Not only did she have to fill the role of mother but also that of the absent, waste-of-space arsehole who had the audacity to call himself my father.

In the first seven years of my life, I had been emotionally formed. My perception of love had been clouded from very early on in life, as I had only really experienced it when it was given to me by my grandmother. When she died, that was it, all over, and I have often wondered just how I would have turned out if she had lived longer. I miss her as much today as I did when I walked out of the Royal Infirmary as a lost little boy in

October 1976. As I grew older, I saw love as something that not only had to be fought for but an environment that had to be fought within, like a psychological boxing ring. Love to me was a Pandora's box of reward and punishment, resulting in confusion, and that is why whilst feeling I had so much to give I also felt unable to show it to those I really did love in case they were taken away from me, my emotions having taken on an oxymoronic aspect. The result of this bewilderment was my attempts to buy love, as I failed to see when it was reciprocated unconditionally. As I entered adolescence and then adulthood, the thing that would always trigger my self-destructive impulses was rejection by a woman.

At the time I was planning to commit suicide by carbon-monoxide poisoning I had, I thought, exhausted every possible avenue of overcoming my flaws and inadequacies and felt that I'd failed to come up with a plan that would afford me the right to carry on living. Love was, and remains to this day, that most elusive of all prizes yet it is also the most accessible if only I knew how to respond to it and accept it. I have consistently pushed those who loved me away whilst inside dearly wanting and needing to let them in and keep them for ever, to love them back the way I know I can if only I could discard the shackles of my past.

I geared up for what I planned would be my last-ever Christmas with an unprecedented enthusiasm, spending more money than ever before. In October, I had already bought Rebekah a car as an early Christmas present and I went absolutely nuts as I drove from retail park to shopping mall day after day, armed with wads of cash. Spending had always been my way of demonstrating my true feelings to the people I loved. Throughout the period when I had money to splash around, both Rebekah and Kerry just had to drop the most subtle of subtle hints and I would go out and get them whatever it was they had said they 'liked'.

I had lost all sense of reason and the money, easy as it was to come by, meant nothing to me other than as a means to put a smile on the faces of my loved ones on the morning of my Christmas swansong. At the final count, I spent, not including Rebekah's car, well over £10,000 on gifts alone and another £1,500 on trimmings, and I threw a few grand at Rebekah and Kerry for nights out and in Rebekah's case so that she could buy presents for others. I gave the boys, aged nine and six, £100 each so they could go shopping to buy presents of their own choosing for other people. I even spent £500 on a huge, oversized promotional model of Sulley from *Monsters Inc.* for Amy, who wasn't even three at the time. This was the kind of thing that truly epitomised what I had become – larger than life, with everything in extreme excess and nothing in moderation: I drove a too-big car, I drank too much, I smoked too much, I took too many drugs, I ate too much, I spent too much. All in all, I was too much and I knew it.

Christmas Day itself was nothing more than a frantic dash between Rebekah's, my flat (which looked like Santa's workshop), then to Kerry's and on to my sister's and finally back to Rebekah's, where, as tradition dictated, I prepared the usual multi-course meal. I was counting down the days to my death.

Initially, I had planned to die on the evening of 30 December. As I set about putting my plans into action, I had to fight against the many thoughts and memories of the year that was drawing to an end, not all of which were unpleasant. I was allowing myself the luxury of a hint of doubt, of an uncertainty that I would have to work hard at overcoming. The memories would flash indiscriminately into my head at the most unlikely of moments. The more I tried to consciously disassociate myself from these lighter thoughts, the more vivid they would become.

All through that week, I spoke to no one except shop assistants in the many chemists where I bought sleepers and painkillers. Two nights before my chosen appointed hour, I made a final purchase of durable rubber piping and an adjustable steel clamp to affix the hose to my car's exhaust. I moved around with the precision of a pre-programmed automaton as I went about my mundane daily routine with little fuss and even less interest. My blackened heart, heavy with defeat and bursting with raw, decaying, unseen emotion, perfunctorily thumped away in my chest as no one noticed anything untoward in my behaviour, not Rebekah, not Kerry and none of my workmates, whose presence I barely registered as I went through the motions the next day for what I had intended to be the final day at my now-despised part-time job.

35

Death Kit

29 DECEMBER 2002

I am alone and I am weeping. I sit in the darkened football arena under the starry winter sky. I have invested many dreams and hopes in this field over many years but now I no longer have any dreams or hopes left to invest. Alone: alone in a cavernous beast of steel, concrete, glass and cheap plastic seats that cost so much – all numbered to assist the hard-of-thinking. But I'm the one who is finding it hard to think. Too hard. Far too hard. As hard as the tears that have frozen into my greying crisp beard. I cannot think, for if I do, I cannot escape what is being said. I strain not to hear but I am no match for the demons.

I am still.

And yet I am still falling.

Why must I always fall?

I am walking. Walking and falling, moist-eyed and blind. I am walking along a cinder path that crunches in time with my unsteady footsteps. I am oblivious to all, yet I am focused. I have a task to perform, a task that I am driven to perform above all else, a task that will remove the focus and take me into the comfort of pure oblivion with nothing beyond. I have a dull ache in my head that I cannot leave behind in this theatre of dreams, and so I will take it with me to a place where it can no longer hurt me.

I am shuffling towards the only exit that I know is left in operation and I hear footsteps approaching me from the darkness I am headed into. I brush past the stranger, who utters some words I do not register, and unacknowledged I leave him in my wake, standing staring at me, looking perplexed as I move towards the goal: my goal. I will learn later that the stranger is a man I once considered to be my friend – a few days ago, which might have been a lifetime ago.

Nothing matters except for my task. This time, I am prepared. I have planned for this event meticulously, even bringing it forward a day as I feel I am ready, more ready than ever, to fall blissfully, painlessly into a relieving nothingness. I have practised and studied the means to this end and I believe strongly that I have finally found my way out. My plans have ensured I will feel no pain in my body. I can no longer tolerate physical pain but I so much need to slip away. The pain in my soul is enough to consider and it is this pain that is driving me towards my lifetime's desire. There will be no bloodshed or shattered limbs on this occasion; I have learned my lessons well. I am not scared so long as I am safe in the knowledge that my body will not experience the same pain I feel in my mind.

It is time.

Time I wasn't here.

Time to go.

I am driving. Driving to a place that is important to me. A place that was once important to us. The place where we first joined together in a physical union that I believed transcended sex. Intervening years have not changed this place. The time of my life has passed and inside I mirror this barren, desolate, winter-ravaged landscape. For her, though, there is the promise of a summer, bringing with it bright light and lush fields. For me, there will be only a frozen darkness, as the sun does not shine on the damned.

Instinctively, I kill the engine. It is vitally important to me that even the most minute details are observed. Appreciating the silence, I pull a canvas holdall from the back seat onto my lap. The silence is broken by the exaggerated rasp of the zipper yielding to my eager movements. It is time. There is no time. No time to lose and, as I tick the boxes on my mental checklist, I throw the doubt of catastrophe back into the bag as it is loudly resealed.

Shut.

Sleeping tablets – 5 packs – 100 units
Ibuprofen and Codeine – 5 packs – 120 units
Vodka – 1×1-litre bottle – 45% abv
1 industrial hose – rubber – 8 metres
1 hose clamp – adjustable for affixation to metallic cylindrical piping

These are items I purchased less than 24 hours ago. Less than £75 in all for my death kit. Not much for a life. I am familiar with this feeling yet it does not seem a natural part of me. It is horrible, hopeless, isolating and agonising. It is an invader that I cannot eject. To flush this anguish away I must flush my whole being away. No longer can I co-exist with this monster. It must die and I as its host must do likewise.

I am outside the car, kneeling in the thickening freezing soil as I carefully, methodically connect the long rubber pipe to the vehicle's waste pipe, the pipe still hot. Fastidiously, I feed the opposite end of the tube into the precisely measured gap I have left open in the rear off-side window of the large all-purpose vehicle that is here, stationary and safely off-road. The vehicle will serve my purpose well. A purpose it was not designed for but one for which it is perfectly suited nevertheless. It is now a vehicle of death and one in which my own journey will terminate. I am glad of the versatility of this vehicle.

My blank expression as I look out over the city betrays nothing of the storm behind my eyes. The storm intensifies gradually, becoming darker, more powerful and more rampant as the chemicals I ingest begin to take control. The storm breaks free from its internal constraints and defiantly, before I cannot operate my body, I turn the key. The engine roars from its slumber and bats and birds scatter, disturbed by the abrupt intrusion, causing me to gasp in fright. Now there is fear.

Through a break in the clouds that envelop my mind, I panic. I have forgotten something. Think. I can't think, as the terrifying rumble emanating from the open end of the hose just behind me is overwhelming. Think. Think about what? My short-term memory is fusing. The rumble is confusing. Think. Oh yes, fuck, forgotten. Think. Hard. Harder. Yesss. Get the bag.

I open the holdall and reach inside for the tiger-printed towel I know is inside and which I can identify by touch alone. The noise at my shoulder is getting louder and now it conjures up images of a long, slow, agonising death. The Grim Reaper merrily increases the tempo of the diabolic dance reverberating in my ears, my heavy sobs slipping unnoticed into its rhythm. The towel? Jam it in the window and expel the cold life-saving air.

I open the car door and fall into the cold earth directly outside. The frightening noise abates. I am shivering and disorientated. That noise is the noise of all my nightmares. Fuck, I don't think I can do this. All my research has been a waste of time. They might know the mechanics of a physically pain-free death but they don't tell you how it will feel. Really feel. How you will feel. They are not me. Fuuuuuuuuuuck!

I get to my feet, telling myself to ignore the constant evil droning. It's only a noise, it can't hurt me (oh yes it can). I rise, trembling, to my feet, frantic with panic, eyes wide open, unblinking. I am in the car again (how did I get back inside?). I cannot escape the noise of my nightmares but I need the source of the noise to send me peacefully away into a permanent sleep without those nightmares. There is no way out.

Another noise, a high-pitched electronic squeal. The remains of my conscious self concentrate hard on answering the telephone (I don't want to die; I just don't want to live). Perhaps I told her of my plans earlier. I don't recall seeing her but that counts for nothing. As I focus on appearing normal in the here and now, I recall very little. She wants to know where I am. I do not tell her. I cannot. She screams tearfully, she is shocked, moved even; she feels guilt but she does not tell me this. I recognise from her inflection that she is human and I have hurt her, although that was not part of the plan. She demands that I tell her where I am but I truly cannot. Physically, my mouth is unable to form

195

coherent sounds (noises) now that the evil brew of alcohol, drugs and the CO gas is rushing through my bloodstream. I open the car door and gulp in the fresh air urgently, the phone still held to my ear. Now I concentrate again. She asks me through her own muffled sobs what I have done and where I am, and this time, defeated and deflated, I surrender to her power yet again and slur to her everything she wants to know. And then I drop the phone.

I am confused and bewildered and I am crushed. I am screaming, wailing like a metamorphosing wolf baying painfully towards the white moon that controls it. I am back in the car. My thoughts do not form completely, fading away and back again in another guise. I am broken, broken down. Why am I like this? Why do I do this to myself? There is no escape. I cannot be mended as I feel the fury of this state coursing a stagnant stream of frustration and into the hollow shell that is (was) my body and soul; the torture of not wanting to live but not wanting to die is agonising as I crumple. Broken, battered and buckled, the only thought that flows through the haze is one of need. As the tremors increase in my shoulders, gradually creeping and encapsulating my whole body, I need to be held. Held tightly in the way a protective mother holds her son (I need my mum). I need to be loved, to be embraced and squeezed so tightly that the demons can be purged from their lair deep inside me. I need to be consoled by an angel but I do not recognise angels when they appear to me. I need my angel. I need what I need. I no longer feel love or hate. I do not love. I do not hate. I feel nothing, for that is what I am.

Nothing.

36

Failure

2003

I didn't achieve my aim.

An obvious statement but the reason for my being unable to finally end my physical existence still surprises even me.

During my shift, I had internally whipped myself up into a frenzy of suicidal negativity, so much so that I made the snap decision to bring forward my intended death by a day. When I finished my shift and gathered my thoughts, I drove to Rebekah's, discarded my work clothes and the usual large wad of recently plundered cash, and within five minutes or so dressed in casual gear and made the trip to the place where Kerry and I had first been together, a place that with my over-romanticised sense of occasion I considered symbolic. I had taken what really should have been a lethal cocktail of alcohol, sleepers and painkillers but I hadn't reckoned on my high tolerance of the drugs. It wasn't until I fired the ignition and heard the aggressive roar of the extended exhaust pipe thundering in my ears that the doubts started to fill me with fear. The drugs exaggerated my thinking processes and gradually I began to dismantle the various stages of dying.

Too many questions.

Would I feel it? Would my heart go first? Would I feel it? Would

197

I choke? Would I feel it? Would my lungs collapse? Would I feel it? Would I just fade away? Would the pain be bad when all my organs imploded? Would I feel it? Would I feel it?

The panic rose through me from the soles of my feet all the way through my body, the combination of drugs slowing my body down yet quickening my mind as they played games with my short-term memory.

I was discovered semi-conscious on the frozen soil beside the wide-open driver's door of my car by an ambulance crew and a police officer who had responded to a 999 call made by Kerry after she had spoken to a largely incoherent me on the mobile before I had lost complete control and collapsed. The memory of those few hours is very cloudy but I do recall clearly the terror I had of the excruciating noise emanating from the open end of the pipe. I couldn't go through with it, unable to overcome my own, surprisingly strong, survival instinct – something I had completely overlooked. It was in that moment, crazed with frustrated perplexity at my incompetence, that I knew, along with everything else that I had failed in, I would forever be unable to take my own life, the only thing that was truly mine to take.

I had been hurting myself, physically and emotionally, consciously and subconsciously, for most of my life but when it came to following through a properly developed plan designed to end my life, I was unable to do even that. Trying to die was not the same as trying not to live. I just wanted to go to sleep and never wake up.

I awoke in the early hours, initially disorientated, in a dimly lit, freezing cold hospital ward, lying under a single, stiff, white cotton sheet without a stitch of clothing. It took me a while to get my bearings but from the livery sewn into the pillows and bedcovers I saw that I was, as I had been in the August of 1990 after my first real suicide attempt, back in Edinburgh Royal Infirmary.

I pressed the button on my bedside handheld console and waited until a small, stern, squat female approached my bed. She flatly refused to give me my clothes even as I shivered with cold under the inadequate thin sheet, offering me another sheet instead and telling me all my possessions, clothes, keys and a small amount of money had been locked away for 'safe keeping'. As she turned away and walked towards the main doors of the ward, I noticed that she used an electronic key to open them and my brain, befuddled with drink and drugs, went into overdrive as I strongly believed that I was on a locked ward, having been sectioned.

Flashes of the ambulance and police involvement started to infiltrate my mind. What had I said to them? What had they said to the hospital staff? As it was, I hadn't been sectioned and after breakfast time I was given my clothes in a crumpled pile and invited to go. No discharge forms, no follow-up appointment.

It was half past nine on a freezing, dreich Monday morning and I stood, quite bewildered, shivering my bollocks off, the cold temperature exaggerated by the still-considerable level of toxicity in my bloodstream and by my lack of a jacket, waiting for a taxi. A few drivers, on seeing my dishevelled, underdressed appearance, refused to stop for me, probably thinking I was an escaped lunatic, as indicated by the white plastic name band hanging from my hypothermic wrist.

Eventually, a cabbie desperate enough for a fare returned me to the back of beyond where my car sat, cold and locked, exactly where I had parked it only 15 hours earlier. The shiny black rubber hose lay innocently at the rear of the vehicle like a recently overpowered vicious python. I pressed the remote button on the car key fob and got in. The car was a mess, littered with empty drug packets and reeking of alcohol. Ignoring the clutter, I turned the key in the ignition, still rather ropey from the effects of the drugs, and jumped inwardly at the noise of the engine firing back into life. I was in no fit state to operate this machine but I had to get away from there as fast as I possibly could. The inbuilt survival impulse of the human condition had been too powerful for me to overcome.

Somehow I managed to navigate my way through the heaving city-centre traffic, concentrating so hard that I could feel the veins on my temples pulsating. I hoped that when I arrived at Rebekah's the house would be empty but hearing the sounds of domestic normality as I turned the key in the front door I knew I was out of luck. Without announcing my arrival, although my car would have been heard, I sneaked upstairs, locked myself in the bathroom and stood under a lukewarm shower for as long as I could. Armed with a set of earplugs and with a very empty heart, naked and alone, I threw myself on Rebekah's double bed and hid myself away from the world. As I entered that place between sleep and wakefulness, I sensed the bedroom door open and Rebekah appeared briefly and told me to phone my friend, the line manager, as apparently he had been concerned at my behaviour the previous day. That was all she said before she turned and slammed the door.

I fell into a deep chemical sleep and awoke in the early evening to an empty house and a huge amount of guilt. Dressing quickly in the dark, I grabbed a wedge of £500 and stuffed it hastily into a brown manila envelope. As I got into my car, intending to drive to Kerry and apologise with the gesture contained in the package, I noticed for the first time since the previous night's escapades that the petrol gauge told me that the tank I had filled only 24 hours earlier was virtually empty, yet I had driven less than 50 miles. I had given it a damn good go on the killing field. It had been more luck than good judgement that had ensured my survival.

After refilling the motor, I drove to Kerry's. She answered the door and stood aside silently as I sheepishly entered. I didn't stay long. I handed her the money, telling her to use it for the holiday I knew she had booked and drained the cup of coffee she had made. I made a lame excuse to save us both more discomfort and left.

As I drove away towards nowhere in particular, she phoned me to thank me for the money and said she would like to meet up with me the next day, my 34th birthday, with the girls, to give me my presents. We agreed on a time and a place and then the line between us was silent for an age before it finally went dead.

Another birthday, one I genuinely hadn't expected to endure and another day in which I would pretend to anyone who enquired that all was well in my world. With the New Year imminent, I would resolve to take each day as it came.

37

The Final Descent

2003–04

With the start of the New Year came a new strength from Rebekah as she demanded that I move out permanently to the Gorgie flat. I had no argument with her reasoning and there were no histrionics. I still had a key for her place and it was made clear that I was welcome at her home any time, that we would remain close friends and that there would be no divorce. She was adamant about the divorce situation.

On two occasions in the spring of 2003, I took massive overdoses of painkillers, sleepers and some of my mum's prescribed medication. These overdoses were the extreme form of what had become my coping mechanism and were not suicide attempts or even 'cries for help'; they were something I can't put a name to. Even with the first waves of calm distortion washing through me I felt no fear of death. The overdoses were just a way in which I could run away and bury my mind, body and soul in the sand, and if I went to sleep without ever waking up, then that would be an added bonus. I also found myself actually enjoying the physical process of my brain shutting down, losing track of time as I fought against the onrushing current of a very deep sleep. Dangerously, I loved the hit this new combination of drugs gave me. I was an addict. But at the time it was still no big deal; I was in control.

During the course of the year, my part-time job became even more part-time. All I cared about as I drove across the city after a shift was getting into the flat and satisfying the nagging craving my body required to feel better about everything. One night, I took 24 tablets in one go – the highest single dose yet – and waited for it to regulate my being. On an empty stomach, it didn't take long and I luxuriated in its warmth. But as the year drew to a close, the ongoing problems with my legs led to a well-founded fear that my addiction might be about to be uncovered.

I had received a letter informing me that I was to attend the Royal Infirmary early in February 2004 for some pre-operation medical tests. By this time I knew that I was to go in for two operations, one in March, which was to be a simple exploratory procedure, with the main operation scheduled for mid-June. The requirement for these tests intrigued me, as they were to ascertain whether or not I would be considered 'fit' for my operations. I wondered just how fit I had to be in order to be considered unfit enough to be made fit again. I was only too aware that the large quantities of drugs I was regularly ingesting must have created some medical anomalies that would be exposed under stringent scrutiny. I thought I would be exposed for the addict I was and I only had a few weeks to attempt to reverse the damage that I was sure I had done, even though I felt very little, if any, pain apart from that in my legs. Rather than addressing the situation, however, I buried my head in the sand and continued in the same reckless vein. If the tests showed any significant telltale signs of my dependence, I would deal with it then. Tomorrow was a much better option than today.

My relationship with Kerry had continued to be as rocky as ever but in an attempt to salvage the situation we had decided to try for another child. I suppose we reckoned that it would be the glue that could perhaps be used to mend the many cracks that had formed over the years. I wasn't really interested in taking another journey along the path of parenthood but for some reason or other I feigned enthusiasm. Perhaps a deeply buried part of me was happy to go along with the baby thing. In any case, she had fallen pregnant and the baby was due at the end of January 2004. Unsurprisingly, Rebekah was unimpressed by the news.

On the day that Kerry went into labour, I called the hospital many times once I knew that she had been admitted but the same hostile midwife barely gave me the time of day. True to form, I got tanked up with tablets and stayed in the Gorgie flat in a miserable, guilt-ridden stupor. I was about to become a father again and instead of being there I had chosen to be alone. It was the first time I recall ever crying myself to sleep but my rest was soon shattered by the ringing of the phone. I chose to ignore it, preferring to take the easy option and listen passively to the message that the blinking red eye on the phone informed me had been left. I was ashamed to speak to Kerry; I had fucked up again and nothing would change the fact that I had missed that most unique of events – the birth of a child. At 00:47, I checked the message.

I had another son.

It was days later that Kerry came to visit me at the flat with our baby, the first time I had set eyes upon him. I held his small, silent, underweight form in the crook of my left arm as I used the other to make a coffee for his proud mum. Without outwardly giving anything away, I instantly fell in love with this baby. But, riddled with conflicting emotions that were further clouded by the omnipresent dulling effects of the chemicals in my body, instead of just giving vent to this instantaneous feeling and being honest, I was downright nasty and cruel as I rained down caustic remark upon caustic remark. Though I never raised my voice, every word was laced with poison and became increasingly vicious, the diatribe delivered while I continued to hold on to my son. After no more than half an hour, Kerry gathered up the innocent bundle and left. I had overstepped the mark, as I could see she was fighting back the tears. Perhaps, in hindsight, the competitive element in our relationship overrode everything else and I had seen her visit as a challenge, nothing more than a point-scoring exercise that, being on my home soil, I just had to win. The solution? More drugs. What else?

After the birth of Aaron, Rebekah understandably went fairly cold on me and so the next few months were spent alone or at work. Because of

203

the drugs, I was now a very insular, sombre individual who was finding it increasingly difficult to don a mask of respectability.

The (un)fitness test I underwent at the hospital resulted in my being assessed as a borderline risk for any surgical procedure to be conducted under anaesthetic. My heartbeat was erratic and my blood pressure way too high, so high in fact that the cardiologist referred to me as 'guaranteed stroke material'. My diet was a disgrace, resulting in my being back on planet obese. I never took even the lightest of exercise and I knew I smoked too much, but what I couldn't admit to the hospital people was that I was taking tablets in huge quantities. I knew beyond any doubt at all that my drug-taking was having a seriously detrimental effect on my body and I also knew for sure that I couldn't stop.

My treatment was allowed to proceed with caution and I was told to present myself for pre-operation investigation. I only had a few weeks in which I could make a token attempt to regulate my body. I had researched opiate withdrawal and I really didn't fancy it one little bit, so I resolved to wean myself off the drugs after I had had my operation. I would, however, have to be extremely careful and deceitful in the meantime, particularly in the event of any medical meddling. I had entered into the next phase of classic addict behaviour.

That March I was not operated on but underwent a pre-op exploratory procedure under local anaesthetic. I was to return in June and was discharged with a wee blue plastic bag bursting with the promise of a cracking weekend. I went to the toilet and got started on pure, unadulterated dihydrocodeine. Consumed with drug-fuelled omnipotence, I had a read of a car magazine and saw a people carrier I fancied, viewed it and handed over well into five figures cash without really paying the slightest bit of attention.

While I was out of action the day after the procedure, I had to leave the criminal side of my activities in the hands of two people: one was a guy I had brought in to be my protector, while the other, my assistant, was a person I considered worthy of the level of trust required to carry out the complicated operation accurately and without fuss. The whole thing ran smoothly without me that day, which only served to prove to me that I was dispensable. Once I went back, one of the major problems encountered during every shift was the severe staff shortages, as many people just didn't bother to turn up. Add to this equation the low quality of staff that did show up and you have a recipe for potential disaster. I was doing the work of too many people and the stress was beginning to show.

In the run-up to my operation in June, things were getting worse all round. On more than one occasion, I found myself hunched over the nearest toilet violently vomiting and crying my eyes out through pure stress. Soon, the drugs had virtually taken hold of most of my life. I was behaving erratically, to the extent that I was taking needless risks at work. I could see my life slipping away from under my feet. One evening, I took 96 over-the-counter painkillers and a further 30 of my mum's prescription painkillers, which resulted in my crumbling in a demented heap. I was screaming in bone-breaking vexation as I became consumed by the desperation that the drugs had at one time protected me from. I slipped into unconsciousness on the floor in the flat, pleading for help.

Another night, I took 126 tablets in less than three hours but, once again, upping the stakes in my drug abuse failed to give me any euphoria. The drugs had simply stopped working. Realising that I was neither dead nor dreaming, I stumbled through to the sitting room, made a coffee and decided there and then to stop taking the drugs. Frightened as I was of the pain of withdrawal, I knew I couldn't go on the way I was. I looked at the clock and it told me that it was 4 a.m.

The first thing I had to do was ensure that I wasn't alone for any length of time and so as soon as the hour became respectable I phoned Rebekah, admitted my problem and asked her if I could come and spend the next few days with her, knowing that the first 72 hours are crucial in avoiding the highly probable relapse. Rebekah told me that she had been aware of my addiction for a while but had been waiting for me to face up to it myself.

The effects of withdrawal would not kick in for at least a full day or so owing to the huge quantities I had taken, so on the way over to Rebekah's I stopped off at a city-centre pharmacy where I was unknown and purchased the strongest over-the-counter sleepers and the strongest anti-diarrhoea preparation available. I was preparing myself for the worst. But the worst was something no chemical agent could overcome.

I got through my first drug-free shift reasonably unscathed and on the way home I began to feel as if I was coming down with a heavy cold but nothing more serious than that. But after the next shift, I woke at Rebekah's dripping in sweat with the bedclothes knotted around me. As I felt my senses come online, I was aware of an overwhelming sensation of nausea washing through my whole body. I got up and bent over the toilet bowl, waiting for the vomit to come. It never did, probably because I had deliberately not eaten. All I would allow myself to take in for at least three days was preventative medication and water, but I was just staving off the inevitable. To a non-addict, opiates constipate the bowels temporarily but with increased use the body becomes accustomed to the drug and so bowel function gradually becomes normalised. My movements were regular and unremarkable but that was with the chemical ever-present in my system. Within hours of opiate deprivation, stomach cramps ensue as the bowels have to evacuate their liquefied contents urgently.

The first time I soiled myself was later on that night as I coughed violently in Rebekah's bed, the force of my coughs being far too powerful for my weakened anal sphincter to match. 'Fuck, I've shit myself,' I thought as I dragged the manky bedclothes from the bed, wet shit covering both my legs. Rebekah took control and, with no protestations whatsoever, took the filthy linen from me, threw it in the washing machine, remade the bed and gently encouraged me to get back in after I had stood under the shower and changed. This was pretty much the order of the next few nights, nights that seemed far worse than the daylight hours, although I had lost all sense of real time.

Committing a technically difficult crime, within tight time constraints and where numerical accuracy is all-important, is a fucking difficult thing to do at the best of times, but in the throes of drug withdrawal it takes on nightmarish proportions. However, by the time the end of shift four arrived, somehow I had managed it and got over the worst. In three days, I had overcome, with the help of Rebekah, some serious physical and psychological adversity, and while I wasn't completely out of the woods, I was certainly over the worst of it. What's more, with a 48-hour break to look forward to, I was £4,000 better off.

For the next three weeks or so, I experienced the last and most irritating part of the drugs departing my body. Obviously, because of their powerful analgesic qualities, opiates attack and numb the nerve endings and pain receptors. The aftermath of the more traumatic withdrawal symptoms involves the return of normal sensation. Pain that the addict is unaware of suddenly becomes magnified and horrendously agonising, and the numbed nerve endings slowly become re-activated, resulting in an inescapable inner itch that feels like millions of tiny insects are trying to eat their way out from the inside, crawling around as they do so. Like the pain, this sensation was much more accentuated during the night and seemed to be never-ending. All the shaking and scratching and changing position made not a jot of difference – all I could do was grin and bear it.

38

Bad Things Coming

2004

During this period, contact with Kerry, for a while at least, was kept to an absolute minimum as I attempted to rebuild my relationship with Rebekah, and this time, I told myself, it would be for keeps. I knew how I truly felt and now, with my senses recently re-sharpened without the opiate clouds in my mind, I was, initially at least, pretty happy with how things were turning out.

But addiction is a difficult thing to overcome and soon, despite the hell of withdrawal that I had been through, I slipped back into taking the pills, though I managed, at first, to keep my intake down to between 12 and 24 tablets a day in the run-up to my next hospital stay.

Rebekah drove me up to the hospital to be admitted before the operation that was scheduled for the following day. Once I was officially processed, she left me to it and returned home. I was told that I was to have a series of blood tests and the results would determine whether or not it would be safe to proceed with the operation. I was panicking that my resumed addiction would be discovered but I put it down to being nervous about my imminent operation: total fucking bollocks given that I was a veteran of around 30 separate surgical procedures and usually took the whole thing in my heavily impeded stride.

Later that day, I tried to kill some time by reading and when that failed I pulled a pen and paper from my bag and tried to write about my feelings. It didn't work at that time, so I asked permission to go off the ward for a while. I had to be alone and I needed a cigarette. All that evening, I nervously flitted between ward and car park, smoking furiously until about 1 a.m., the time the bloods came back. I was astonished when the solitary night nurse informed me that the results showed no anomalies whatsoever.

The next day, I awoke from the anaesthetic with only the dullest of throbbing pain in my right ankle. But the effects of the recovery drugs faded fast and the pain set in. Four hours after my operation, a pair of stainless-steel crutches were thrown at me and I was informed that I was to get up and walk as soon as possible. Not in the mood to offer any form of protest, I slowly and carefully edged my body to the side of the bed and swung my legs over. There, I momentarily froze as I looked down at the operation site. Over the wound was a heavyweight plaster-of-paris knee-high cast and in the area of the ankle there was a large, outward-spreading, still wet, misshapen, maroon-coloured circle, darker and wetter in the centre. Ignoring the physio, I alerted a nurse to the presence of this seepage but was told that it was normal and would be cleaned before my leg was put into a lightweight cast prior to my discharge. It didn't look normal to me and I had seen my legs in similar circumstances many times before. I reckoned I knew better but I accepted what I was told and just got on with it.

Ignoring the searing pain underneath the burgundy blemish, I slipped the crutches onto my arms, got up tentatively, shaking a bit at first before settling my weight on my left leg, and walked. It had been ten years since I had used elbow crutches but, like riding a bike, within a few hesitant minutes I found a bit of the old form. One thing I hadn't accounted for, though, was my lack of general fitness. I was 18 stone, with very high blood pressure and a huge fag and drug habit, and so very soon sweat soaked the whole of my upper body.

I was discharged on the Monday and with Rebekah driving all I was interested in was the bag of prescribed drugs I had stuffed into my case. I just wanted to get to Rebekah's and tank myself up.

That first night out of hospital was awful. I had to crawl on all fours to get up and down the stairs and toiled to manoeuvre myself around the many obstacles disguised as innocent household items with my cumbersome crutches. After taking too many of my discharge drugs, I felt extremely sick and was unable to make it to the toilet in time, instead vomiting violently at the bedside.

A few days later, when I was back in my flat, Rebekah went on holiday and I spent 15 days on my own, going out only to buy drugs. None of my so-called 'mates' came anywhere near me, Kerry was still keeping well out of my way and I was frantic with demented loneliness by the time Rebekah came back. I was back to taking 24 to 36 tablets a day.

As the weeks after my operation rolled on, the pain in my leg only slightly abated and it turned out that an infection had set in due to the fact that the wound had not been cleaned in the vital 48 hours immediately after the operation. I was treated with antibiotics but the whole healing process had been severely arrested by the avoidable infection.

At nine weeks post-op, against all the advice I had been given, I went back to my part-time job. I didn't go for the money and I didn't go out of fear that the fraud would be discovered – confident as I was in the ability of the person I had appointed as my assistant. I went because my friend the line manager had been withdrawn from the operation to work in another area and his replacement had apparently pleaded for me to be there as I was familiar with the staff and idiosyncrasies of the client. I was told I would just be there for the sake of being there and assured that I wouldn't be required to do anything that would compromise my physical weakness; I would in effect just be an adviser. It was on this understanding that I strapped myself up without my carbon-fibre splint and drove to work two months before I should have been anywhere near the place. Putting myself out through a sense of misguided loyalty to a company I had grown to dislike intensely was to prove a very costly error of judgement indeed.

That day at work was hell on earth as I struggled to deal with the sheer agony spreading throughout my whole body from the tender, unhealed, raw wounds in my leg. At the end of the day, I removed my shoe and sock and the layers of strapping from my leg and saw that not only had my ankle swollen to twice its size but the edges of the wound had slightly split apart. I sat down, not on a chair but on a desk, elevated the offending limb as best I could and contacted my boss for the day and told him I was going home. I hobbled out to my car, blood pissing out from the hem of my black trousers, and did just that.

I needed drugs, this time to address the pain, and I needed more than anything else to lie down. Deep down inside, I was only too aware as I drove back to the flat that I had fucked up again.

Sure enough, at my next hospital visit, I learned that the procedure had not been as successful as hoped. The operation had failed but, feeling ashamed and guilty at disobeying the surgeon's strict convalescing instructions, I told him that I felt better than I had before the procedure. I couldn't tell him the truth. I had undone all his good work and professional investment in me.

Over the next few weeks, I did the sensible thing and stayed away from work, although on one occasion I ran the criminal side of the operation from the comfort of my living room. It was all going wrong more quickly than I knew but I had a few other pressing issues to deal with. My ever-convoluted love life was nearing the point of no return. At last, some sort of conclusion would be reached.

In the first week of October, after a week-long highly abusive text session, both Kerry and I, independently of each other, changed our contact phone numbers. It had been coming for a while. After the confrontation following Aaron's birth, we had re-established contact but only for the sake of the kids and in a very businesslike manner.

On one of the very few occasions when I was at Kerry's during this period, handing over a wedge of cash, she summed me up by saying coldly, 'When you are being nice you are the most loving, romantic man any woman could ever want, but when you are fighting, you are positively evil.'

She'd have to live with it – I did.

39

Numb

2005

I saw the New Year in alone in the flat, drugged up to the eyeballs. I was lonely and melancholy, and no amount of chemicals could alleviate my sadness. The drugs I was taking had now become an integral part of my self. I couldn't function without them in my system.

I was by now way out of control, taking my first handful of drugs within two hours of wakening and the remaining thirty-six staggered at various times throughout the day. I wasn't getting a hit any more. Managing my habit was becoming a full-time occupation, as I was now known in many of Edinburgh's pharmacies. I had to ensure that I did not visit any of the shops more than once a fortnight, or if I had to go to the same place, I would have to change the times I went and hover around in order to be served by a different shop assistant. By this time, I had already been questioned by two chemists in particular and so I had struck them from my list of 'suppliers'. Often I would get in the car and travel to chemist shops in many of the small towns surrounding Edinburgh (Bonnyrigg, Dalkeith, Penicuik and Musselburgh) and sometimes even further afield to Fife, the Borders or West Lothian. If I happened to be through in Glasgow or maybe Dundee, I would always take the opportunity to nip into a few branches of Boots or Lloyds to keep my reserves up.

I got round many of the pharmacy assistants by telling them that the drugs I was buying were the only things that I found suitable for my condition and I had to buy them as they were not available on prescription (which they weren't) but my GP was aware of what I was doing. This seemed to satisfy most of the girls in the various shops, as many of them had seen me hobbling on my crutches during the summer months, when again I had chosen to 'self-medicate'.

After a highly forgettable New Year's Day shift at my part-time job, I walked away with a £2,000 bulge in my back tail. I got drunk and angry very quickly that night and knew that I had to face up to myself and the mess I had created once and for all. I had told myself this so many times before that even I was sceptical – but I knew I couldn't do it alone. I needed Rebekah.

I went to her house and poured my heart out – there was no façade, no wall to protect myself that night. I lay down beside her and she held me closer than she ever had before, absorbing my pain, taking as much of it as she could from me, soothing my agonised senses and throwing it all to one side. It was 5 a.m. and I knew for sure at that moment, a moment of pure clarity through the fog of the mind-altering cocktail I had consumed, that my future, my life, lay as I did that night with Rebekah. My wife.

A few days later, due to an incident that I am unable to elaborate on, I was arrested on two counts of breach of the peace that were to result in a sentence of 120 hours' community service and 18 months' probation. Added to the fact I had experienced a miserable time in police custody in respect of these offences, all in all it was a very severe sentence resulting from what I would suggest is an immoral abuse of public resources. Unfortunately, an uncomfortable combination of personal circumspection and legal restriction subjugates a deeply held frustration and prevents me from going into further detail about what happened at this point. It is a sad day when even now I am censored in order to protect the vilest of criminal offenders. But accept this I must. For now!

Despite this situation, and even though I was fighting a losing battle against my addiction problem at the time, I clung on to the new optimism I had felt with the dawning of the New Year. I was more determined than I had ever been to get my marriage on a solid, lifelong footing and I was looking forward to leaving the constricting environment of my part-time job and setting up a legitimate, less stressful business venture. The future, for once, looked, if not rosy, then certainly a lot brighter than the past had allowed me to think possible.

When I returned to my part-time job, something had changed inside me. I was tormented, in pain, terrified of what my future would hold, but I did still have that spark of hope shining through. I was still addicted, I was still embezzling, but I had finally reached a point so low that the only thing I could do was move up.

It wouldn't be an easy process.

For the next two months, I barked, swore, sulked, stomped and became as close to tyrannical as I was ever likely to be. I became increasingly pissed off as I went through the motions at work. I knew I had to get out. Turning up for work was becoming nothing more than a tortuous, sapping chore. I was frankly just marking time until the beginning of May, when I knew there would be a natural break in the job and a time when I could safely leave and put my flagging energies into my new business venture, a football memorabilia shop, a venture I had by the beginning of March invested heavily in, spending almost £10,000 in cash on stock and a year's lease on a retail premises near to my flat: a flat that was lying empty most of the time, as I had been back at Rebekah's house.

My relationship with my wife and boys was the only worthwhile part of my life, as everything else was in terminal decline. My drug habit was now being supplemented, once again, with the over-the-counter sleeping tablets I had used for years and which were now available in double-dose-strength pills, and so my total chemical intake was 48 painkillers and 12 to 15 sleepers in every 24-hour period in my life. The normal recommended dose (short-term) was a maximum of eight painkillers and one sleeper. I was at one with the drugs as they were at one with me, but like any addict entering a period of rapid freefall I still believed that I was retaining a modicum of control.

Back at New Year, I had blacked out and since then my memory, both short- and medium-term, had become noticeably impaired. I would be told of things I had said, conversations I had participated in and things I had done, and while I nodded along with what I was being told, trying to pretend I was in possession of a clue as to what people were on about, I could not for the life of me remember. I was in a lot of trouble. It had become so bad at one point that I truly believed many of my work colleagues were conspiring behind my back purely to make my life difficult. This paranoia fuelled my desire to leave my life behind and start over on my own. I felt as though I was at war with the world.

On 5 March 2005, I drove myself to my part-time job for what I didn't know was to be my final shift. Before I checked in for work, I nipped into a nearby supermarket to spend a tenner in its pharmacy and took a couple of tablets in the car before driving the final mile or so to work. I was early, but then I was always early, punctuality being an obsession of mine. Later on that night, I was looking forward to a night out with Rebekah, possibly even booking a hotel if she was up for it. I was really trying to make things work between us and had intended to make a public show of being with her in the pubs and clubs I knew some of my workmates frequented. I was at long last making our relationship 'official' and I wanted to show her off, particularly as she was a stranger to most of the people I worked with. This was meant to be 'our' year and I really wanted to make Rebekah feel special.

Work was busy that day – it seemed as if every senior member of staff was in. On reflection, I really should have smelt a rat but preoccupied as I was with thoughts of my impending night out I went about my duties with a seasonal spring in my step. The first domino was only six hours away from crashing spectacularly and it would set off a chain of events that would result in my hitting the bottom of the darkening pit.

I went about my criminal business as usual, breaking my routine only to go to my car, where I took six tablets. I noticed the senior area manager sitting silently in the passenger seat of his car, which had been parked in such a way as to box me in with only millimetres between his rear bumper and my front one. I didn't really think that there was anything particularly unusual in this, as parking space was always at a premium. Not wishing to appear ignorant and having time to kill, I engaged him in meaningless conversation through the open window of his car. Before I went back into work, he made an odd request. He asked me if I would mind opening the passenger door as he said it was sticking and he couldn't reach out from the inside. I gave it a couple of tests, it seemed fine to me, said cheerio and walked back inside.

From there, I went into the first nearby vacant toilet and emptied my pockets, pouring a pile of banknotes onto the top of the cistern in the locked cubicle. I counted out a total of £1,840 and from that I removed a wad of £300, which I placed in the breast pocket of my jacket, the cut for part of the scamming syndicate. The remaining £1,500 was placed in one of the pockets of my works over-jacket to be split later on between myself and my protector. The £40 I put with another score I had in my front tail, giving me a reasonable sum of £60 that I could explain easily if challenged, not that I was expecting to be at the time. As I walked out the lavvy, I still had no intimation of anything untoward occurring.

With 15 minutes to go until the end of the shift, I was sitting with my protector drinking coffee when I received a message to present myself at the client's main office. Immediately, I knew there was a major problem. I have no idea how I knew; I just did. At the same time, I got wind of two other staff members having been called to the same area, one of whom was a member of the syndicate. In that moment, as the butterflies started spinning big style in my stomach, I realised that after thirteen years of living a charmed life and only two months away from walking away from it for good, my biggest fear regarding the scam had finally happened. Slipping quickly into survival mode, I slowly removed my works jacket and told my protector to lock it away somewhere in my absence. And he did, in one of the safest places imaginable.

Of the three of us pulled in, I was certain I would be resourceful and strong enough not to let anything slip but I had concerns about the one guy who I knew had his cut on him. I was last to arrive at the main office and was held outside in a corridor that also had a smaller ante-room directly opposite the door of the main office. I was initially joined by the senior area manager, who acted all chummy but I knew from his demeanour that he had been part of whatever set-up had brought me to this point. As I spoke to him, my heart sank as I remembered that I had the £300 in my breast pocket and after gathering myself I decided to take a calculated risk. I told him that I was in possession of the money as I had arranged to have a look at something with a view to purchasing it from a fellow staff member for my soon-to-be-opened shop. He said nothing and turned away and walked into the main office. Alone in the corridor, I looked around for somewhere to stash the cash and after a cursory inspection of my surroundings I came up blank. I lit a cigarette in frustrated resignation, trying to concentrate hard on my immediate predicament. If found with £300 on me in mixed-denomination £20s, I was in no position to explain it away easily. It was at this point that I was passed in the corridor by the two other guys as they came out of the ante-room and were led away in between two coppers.

Once again, I found myself alone in the corridor, eyes all over the place looking for a hidey-hole for the rapidly cooking £300 in my pocket. And then I saw it. But I was a microsecond too late. Or was I? It was nearly spin-the-wheel time again. The replacement who had been sent out to keep an eye on me was a man I knew had his own little dodges on the go and I reckoned he thought I knew a lot more than I actually did. Gamble number two involved me first asking him if he would take the cash from me but he refused steadfastly, stammering that he wanted nothing to do with anything. I then told him what I was going to do with it and he shrugged his shoulders as I took a few steps to my left and secreted the dough in one of three fluorescent orange works jackets (the client's, not ours) hanging up on a nearby hook. I asked the guy if he had seen what I had just done and his reply was simply, 'I seen fuck all.' He too was way out of his depth. So far so good but still a long way to go.

Eventually, after escorting the first two guys to the station, the two cops returned and relieved the nervous replacement. He breathed a sigh of relief as he scuttled away into the relative safety of the main office, leaving me at the mercy of the two obviously uninterested cops.

They took me into the ante-room and informed me that I was free to walk away at any time, that I was not under arrest but it had been alleged that I was in possession of a significant sum of cash that I had obtained by fraudulent means. My calm exterior belied the cadaver of jelly I had become inside. They then asked how much cash, if any, I had on me and I told them I had approximately £60 in my pocket as I was meant to be going out for a few drinks with my wife. I was then asked if

I was happy to be searched and I nodded in silent cooperation. During the search, the cops said that they had been told I had £300 on me, to which I replied by asking them if it was the senior area manager who had made the allegation. They asked me why I asked and I said I'd fed him a line to see if he was a grass.

I'd made him look a proper arsehole and it was at that point that I knew for sure that I would walk away from trouble. The cops asked me to accompany them to the small office I shared with the line manager and then to another staffroom in order that they could conduct a thorough search of these areas in my presence. Again, to the bewilderment of the cops, the search was to no avail. My protector had given my stuff, including my jacket with the money in it, to the line manager, as our friendship was well known, and he innocently put it in the back of the company vehicle he had use of, where it was hidden under the noses of everyone. The cops said that I was no longer required and could go, although they said that they might be in touch depending on the outcome of their further enquiries.

I sat in the driver's seat of my car and devoured the rest of the drugs left in the glove compartment before heading to the nearby Asda to buy a fresh pack of pills. I had £63 in my pocket and nothing in the bank. I had embezzled something in the region of £1.125 million and in that time had given a huge amount in various guises, cash and otherwise, to Rebekah and Kerry and others. I had lived an increasingly ostentatious life, buying all sorts of stuff, going nuts at Christmas time, being impulsive, enjoying a four- and five-star lifestyle on various trips and holidays. I had used a lot of it to buy love, friendship and acceptance. The rest, as George Best once said, well, that I just squandered.

The money that I had used for so many years as both my sword and my shield was gone. Now I would be laid bare for all to see – naked, afraid and very vulnerable.

In the immediate aftermath of that night, all those involved in the scam and a few other innocent members of staff were interviewed, or arrested, or lost their jobs – every staff member except one. Similarly, only one person would be charged by the cops with embezzlement. That lucky chap would be me.

On the Monday after my final shift, after 48 hours of frantic phone calls between us all, I arranged a meeting of all those involved. I told them truthfully that I was prepared to take the rap and go to prison if it came to it but that it was also imperative we were all singing from the same song sheet when we were interviewed. Furthermore, it was vitally important to keep each other informed immediately of any information pertinent to our current plight. It was agreed that no matter who asked, it was now a case of keeping all mouths shut and pleading ignorance.

One of the things that worked in my favour was an absolute myth that I was connected to a firm of heavy Edinburgh gangsters. While I never did or said anything to perpetuate this nonsense, I certainly didn't go out of my way to dissuade anyone of its validity. I knew about it and played on it, as I knew people were in real fear, but the nearest I ever got to organised crime was owning a boxed DVD set of *The Godfather*.

I was eventually asked in the summer to present myself for interview under caution at a police station. By this time, my football shop was up and running, and Rebekah had agreed to open up for me until the cops were through with me. I had been assured by the investigating officer when I returned his phone call that even in the event of being charged I would not be held in custody. The interview was an utter farce.

They hit me with a few allegations and I was asked a lot of questions that had no apparent bearing on anything as far as I could see until it was suggested that I was by far more intelligent than any of the others and it was obvious I was the brains behind a huge conspiracy and at the helm of a criminal empire. I replied by saying that if I was so clever then surely I would not be so stupid as to commit an offence while on probation. They had nothing on me and they knew it. The final act of the interview was the police officially charging me with 'embezzlement of an unknown sum of money', and I was asked if I wished to make any reply. I did, and again I answered with a question, 'If it's an unknown sum of money then how can it be proved that it's missing in the first place?' Once the tape was turned off, I added that I would go not guilty all the way as any half-decent lawyer on his day off would tear holes in their inept case. Surprisingly, they both agreed.

40

Baggage

2005

I started my business, a shop selling football memorabilia and books, on the final day of April 2005 and it became obvious very quickly that I had bitten off a far bigger piece than I ever had any hope of chewing. With the choice of remaining at my part-time job on my own terms having been removed, I was without the extra financial resources I had banked on. Before I even opened up, I was playing catch-up, having less than £1,000 to my name. I tried my best to make it work, often working up to 18 hours a day, but it became obvious that I didn't have enough business acumen to be successful with no financial back-up whatsoever; in fact, far from being a candidate for entrepreneur of the year it was soon painfully clear that I was flogging a dead horse. Actually, that would have been an achievement in itself, as it was apparent by then that I would have trouble flogging a glass of water to a dehydrated marathon runner in the middle of a baking desert. It didn't stop me trying, though.

I had realised in the short time I had been trading that the local population comprised a disproportionately high level of weirdos, oddballs and simpletons. Hardly the location in which to make a fortune and so it was patently obvious that the shop alone was not going to generate even close to enough income for me to survive. In an attempt to salvage the situation, I began to trade online. With this string added to my bow, money started to flow in a bit faster, though it meant I had no time for anything else.

The money generated from this source I left in an account for a few months to build up, only to be tapped into in the event of an emergency. I had amassed a fair few quid before the inevitable emergency occurred and I reluctantly dusted off my bankcard and stuck it in the nearest ATM, which spat it back out. I then got a mini-statement from the machine and it informed me I owed the bank the sum of my arranged overdraft. There must have been some mistake, so I went to the branch and asked what was happening.

The chubby young teller was non-confrontational as she told me that the system was right and printed me a more detailed statement. I was incredulous. It was all gone, every last penny I had minus £100-odd in my account. I studied the statement intensely, poring over every single figure, and it slowly became clearer as I realised I had fallen victim to a highly sophisticated computer fraud through my online trading environment. What had gone around had indeed come around and, although I found myself inwardly laughing wryly, I knew for sure that I was finally financially ruined. The crime had been committed in less than an hour from start to finish and had lain undiscovered for a couple of days. The perpetrators were long gone and on a business level all the fight had been knocked out of me. I had fuck all and was on the way to losing even more.

Overnight, I subconsciously gave in and made the decision to stop trying. Yes, I still put in more hours than I should have, not really knowing what else to do as I fumbled around in the dark. The business needed money to survive, I needed money to survive; the more I tried, the more I failed; the more drugs I took, the more drugs I needed to take; the more money I needed, the more money I used from the shop, and the more the business failed. And the more all this happened, the further I withdrew from my life and those I loved.

I was making less than £20 per day and it was going on drugs, fags and cheap shitty food. I knew I looked as awful as I felt but the sad truth was that I no longer cared. Not for me, not for anybody and not for anything. I hated myself more than I ever had.

There was a bright day in the midst of all this as Rebekah graduated with her Humanities degree from the University of Edinburgh. My heart sang a thousand songs of pride that day but, as usual, I said nothing. In fact, I left quickly to open up the shop, even though it would have been rare to actually see a paying customer. All I really cared about came in silver boxes from Boots. The attention I paid to those pills was at the expense of my love for Rebekah.

I had totally neglected her and after what had been a particularly stressful few months, she had been forced to vacate her house and move into a council flat. Even before I entered the place, I was horrified. My family had been reduced to this – living in a shithole in the middle of a slum. I had a quick, silent look round, my expression growing ever sterner as I made my mind up that it was the nightmare of nightmares. I confronted my own failure as a husband, a father and, most of all, a man. This was what I had reduced them to. 'It's a fucking dump,' I told her. She had been through hell: having to move, passing her exams and dealing with my shit, and yet all I could do was criticise. I had done nothing to help her find a decent new place and had offered no support as I was too wrapped up in my own self-inflicted crises. Rebekah had been there for me during my bleakest times but I couldn't reciprocate. She looked so vulnerable and forlorn but I wouldn't even go to her and hold her as I should have done. My days of taking my wife for granted were numbered.

In early November, I climbed down from the saddle of my high horse and held out what I considered to be an olive branch of sorts to Rebekah. I wanted to go over and make peace, and so I sent a light-hearted flirtatious text message to her phone, suggesting we share a long shower in her new place in order to 'christen' it. I was not looking for sexual gratification, just a means to stop the rot that I had been instrumental in creating. This resulted in a text argument with her and it went on until her answer to my text question of 'What now?' was, 'I think a divorce would be best all round.' I ended the argument with, 'I'll wait and hear from your lawyer', only thinking about closing the argument and not believing for a minute it would go anywhere.

She wasted no time. The following Wednesday, I opened a white envelope, the contents of which asked me to return a form to Rebekah's solicitors if I agreed to a quick divorce. She had meant it. I imploded and collapsed in tears in the hall of the flat. I never wanted it to come to this and I really couldn't get my head round it. What the fuck was happening to me? Solution – more drugs.

I was hurting badly. I wrote a hastily constructed, scrawled note written on the back of her lawyer's request, grabbed my wedding ring and stuffed both articles into an envelope on which I scratched the single word of Rebekah's maiden name. After having turned my unfaithful attitude around and behaved myself impeccably for the best part of a year, I couldn't understand why she had done this to me. Yes, my behaviour had been despicable in the past and, yes, the money I had used as a pacifier over the years had run out, but I was truly at great pains to comprehend what felt like the most eviscerating of all betrayals. Such was the acceleration of my descent at that time.

41

Over

2005

My acceleration towards the darkest reaches of the abyss now picked up pace and there weren't enough hours in the day as I filled my time with little more than work, sleep and the consumption of dangerously high levels of over-the-counter sleepers and painkillers. The spontaneous bouts of vomiting had started in late September the year before but as they were sporadic I ignored what my body was trying to shout at me. Even when the vomiting became more frequent and violent, I paid little heed. In the evenings, it would often occur spontaneously as I messed around on the Internet or watched telly and I would expel the contents of my stomach two or three times a night, regularly not reaching the relative safety of the bathroom as I did so. I fought the nauseating impulse, swallowing back the puke, particularly if I had just ingested some pills, and on the many occasions that I was unable to control the liquid projectile spewing forth, I was often to be found on all fours, sifting through the vile bubbling fluid like a gold prospector, searching for any regurgitated tablets, which, once found, would be run under a cold tap and once again, although smaller now, swallowed whole without so much as a twitch. On several occasions, I spewed on the walls, doors, windows and floor of the flat, and that was if I had a wee bit of luck. Most times my vomit would cover several pieces of furniture, the three-piece suite, the computer, the bed and on one occasion I even created a Picasso-esque living picture in puke straight over the fragile screen of my monster television – a possession I had hung on to with grim determination having sold or pawned virtually every other item of value I owned. No more fancy cameras, camcorders, games consoles or laptops. The Internet and phone lines were weeks away from disconnection and I was living, frankly, in a palace of putrefication. My diet, when I kept it down, consisted of cheap, fatty food containing little in the way of proper nourishment. Bills remained unpaid and I would grow to live in fear of every knock on the door. Every penny I made was feeding my addictions and making me fatter. I was a fucking mess.

My chemical intake was massive. I was at my maximum. I was consuming, every day, 72 to 120 over-the-counter painkillers; 10 to 15 double-strength over-the-counter sleepers; 20 DF118s – 60mg (which I had managed to con out of my GP); and 10 to 20 Prozac, which I had been prescribed for depression. Even though I knew intellectually my pill-taking had long since departed the realms of manageability, still I denied I had a significant problem. My life was crumbling yet I plodded on, pretending to the world that all was well.

There was some good news, as the embezzlement case against me had been dropped, declared 'not in the public interest' by the Procurator Fiscal, but rays of sunshine were few and far between.

On Christmas Eve, I went over to Rebekah's flat and in the morning, even though I had tried my best, I felt awful when I saw the lack of parcels, the space underneath the Christmas tree crammed only with emptiness.

The greatest gift Rebekah could have given me that day was her love and an assurance that she had put a halt to the divorce proceedings. That would have meant more than any tangible present. Yes, she had melted a bit but I realised that there was still a long way to go to win her heart back. As the day wore on, I was only biding my time in order to drive to a chemist I knew was open for emergency supplies and that is what I did while, breaking another important symbolic tradition, Rebekah prepared the Christmas meal.

That night, when the boys had gone to the room they now had to share, I tried to make Rebekah see the way I felt about her. To show her that she was the most important, special woman I had ever had the pleasure of knowing. I had married her because I had been in love with her but something, somewhere had been lost in translation. I was trying so hard to finally speak her language.

A few days later, Rebekah had been invited to a New Year party and it was made transparently clear that the invitation did not extend to me, going along as she did with Kearan. Daniel, in a beautiful gesture, elected to see in the bells with his old crap dad at the flat and that meant so much to me. It had taken 11 years for us to become close and, although the business had been an abject failure in every other way, because of his love for football, the shop had at long last brought my firstborn to a place where his dad could love him and form what I hope has become an unbreakable bond.

My son just managed to stay awake to see the back of 2005 and after wishing each other a Happy New Year with big hugs and bigger hopes, he stumbled through to the spare room, where he fell quickly into a deep sleep. Full of drugs but wide awake, I lay atop my own bed, my thoughts disturbed occasionally by the distant cheery echoes of revellers.

I contemplated the year left behind. I had been exposed for the fraudulent human being I had become. I had lost Kerry and my younger kids. I had lost my part-time job with its bonuses. I had lost every penny and item of material value that I owned. I had lost my health and my hold on rationality as a result of all these things. In the midst of all these maudlin musings, as if to underline the extent of just exactly how much I had lost, I was startled back into my reality by my mobile phone declaring the arrival of my first text message of 2006. I opened the message, which was from Rebekah. The circle was nearing completion.

The cold, distant, impersonal, almost random text read simply 'Happy New Year'. A shiver of realisation bristled over my already freezing flesh. I knew in that instant that my marriage was over.

* * *

There was a New Year get-together at Rebekah's brother's organised for the afternoon of 2 January. The day started off well, with me driving our elder son, who had stayed at the flat since Hogmanay, over to his uncle's house, and while he went to get changed into some clean clothes I stood facing Rebekah in her narrow kitchenette. Looking into her eyes, I took her in my arms and as my hands slipped inside the waistband of her jeans we kissed and wished each other a Happy New Year. It seemed so simple and natural a gesture, it seemed so sincere, but it was to be followed by coldness for the rest of the day. When I returned with them to the flat after the party, I headed to the point of no return. For what I was about to do, there would be no forgiveness, and redemption would remain more elusive than ever. But I really didn't plan it like that. The devil within was warming up for an attempt at a new diabolical and ultimately self-destructive record.

I didn't feel any different inside; there were no warning signs. I was feeling as normal as I was ever likely to at the end of what had been a horrendous 12 months. I swallowed the remainder of the tablets I had in my pocket. My total consumption for the day had only been 48 painkillers – around a third of my normal daily intake and not enough to maintain my chemical equilibrium. I was taking it easy, as I knew I would be drinking. The alcohol was perhaps not a wise idea either, as it had been a long time since I had mixed drugs with drink and I was unsure as to the overall effect of the mixture. Or maybe I am looking for excuses to justify the soon-to-be-unleashed frustrated fury that was on a slow burn just below the surface – and climbing. Something had to give and I was in grave danger of losing control. I just didn't know it.

I lay on the settee, resting my head in Rebekah's lap, willing her with all that remained of the good part of me to stroke my forehead, my face, my neck. Anything. She kept her hands neutral, at her sides, on a newspaper, in a jar of Quality Street – anywhere but me.

I felt like nothing. I was nothing.

I wasn't nothing. What was happening in my head?

BANG!

I picked a fight with my wife and she took the bait obligingly. That was that. It was the only excuse I needed; every single sliver of impotent angst exploded in petulant frustration. The devil had just come out to play. Oblivious to anything or anyone in my immediate vicinity, I ranted, I shouted, I screamed in Rebekah's face, bringing up everything that had gone wrong and blaming it on her. It all came out in an asthmatic diatribe. I became increasingly animated and more and more dangerous, and Rebekah, now terrified for her safety, played a card that would either placate me or push me completely over the edge.

She picked up the phone and threatened me with the police, reasoning that because I was still on probation for the unmentionable offence the fear of imprisonment would stop me in my tracks. But she was wrong. I was gone. I had no fear. Not of jail. Not of anything. Relentlessly, I systematically, yet chaotically, destroyed everything in the room, howling through the stream of snot, tears and slavers dripping from my ugly, ugly face.

Then, in the briefest of interludes, I heard a sound that brought me back. Back to a place I had never been. Kearan, who had just witnessed my anger for the first time in his young life, was sobbing, wide-eyed and helpless, as he stood rooted to the spot just inside the half-open door. The sound of his tears stopped the devil in his tracks.

From that moment on, things would never, ever be the same between me and the only child I had ever connected with since birth. If I thought I had lost everything before the day had started, I was sure of it now. In one demonic outburst, the last remaining droplets of the once fast-flowing river of love my wife had offered me for so long evaporated like the cascade of cash had done eight months earlier, evaporated into nothingness, never to flow again. The angel had given her all and more only for the devil to throw it back in her face once too often, desecrating all that they had shared once and for all.

With the anger now subdued and the demons sated, I knew I had no choice. I had to go. Rebekah followed me to the door, her fear having joined my anger. I stood outside on the grey stone-clad floor of the stairwell, gazing silently into my wife's eyes as she impatiently waited for me to turn and leave. Returning her tear-stained yet ever-so-determined stare with a lost, placatory, imploring, childlike stare of my own, I knew part of me, of us, had been killed for ever. Her eyes bored into my soul, my expression that of the vulnerable child I would always be. A lost confused boy, wandering, dazed in the aftermath of chastisement that had been dished out by his mother for reasons he would never fully understand. The child within had been desecrated by the adults charged with his safekeeping, savaged by a past that would not let go.

What had I done?

I had just thrown away the single most important thing I had ever had and in the process destroyed the love that I had to give and needed so much to receive. Where once I had it all, now I truly had nothing. Nothing at all.

Rebekah looked at me and said without emotion, 'I was going to tell you that I was going to stop the divorce.'

The door was then slammed shut in my face.

After that final showdown, whatever it was that was 'in me' dragged me down to the absolute bottom of the blackest pit that even I had previously been unable to imagine.

The game of 'dodge the pharmacy assistant' had become almost impossible, as my geographical boundaries had been severely restricted due to my lack of transport. As I traipsed the streets of Edinburgh on foot, not willing to spend any money on bus fares, preferring to save it to put towards more tablets, I was visiting the same chemist shops too often. Day after day, I wandered around the city centre waiting for the chance to be served by an unknown shop girl or one who hadn't seen me for a few days, becoming more desperate as I did so. I had run out of people that I could ask to nip into a chemists for me if they were passing; nobody wanted to know me any more. As I shuffled through the grey streets, I was alone. Alone in a street full of people. Alone with my weakness and alone with my tormentor-in-chief.

I was unkempt, dirty and shabby. I was past caring about myself. In the six weeks since Christmas, my weight had plummeted by three and a half stone. While the vomiting continued aggressively, I had stopped eating, reasoning that if I had no food inside me I wouldn't feel sick. But it didn't work like that. The puking had become a significant irritation but no more than that. My insides were in a serious mess, as indicated by the fact that I was struggling even to absorb water – water that I needed to accompany my drugs, not to keep me alive. Remaining alive was not foremost in my thoughts, as I already felt like a dead man limping – limping from chemist to chemist in a parody of a postie's delivery run.

On the last day I took my drugs, I was challenged by an older, silver-haired shop assistant with a disdainful look of disapproval etched into her features. She reluctantly sold me that final pack of tablets but made it clear she was unhappy about it. As I added the packet to the three others in my inside pocket, I was struck by a feeling of guilt, remorse, self-loathing, fear and at long, long last, realisation. The bulge in my pocket would indeed be my final hit.

Reality came rushing towards me: I had been the author of my own misfortune. The lies, the infidelity, the stealing, the violence, the cheating, the using and abusing, the arrogance and defiance – I was seeing myself as others had seen me, as my wife had seen me, the angel I had violated and whose love I had desecrated in a drink- and drug-fuelled fury of uncompromising selfishness. I had performed an act of destruction that not only ended my relationship with my wife but also imprinted an unforgivable demonic transfer onto the minds and souls of my two older boys – my real friends. I had the full set now. I had alienated everyone I had ever loved. My anger – in me from early childhood – had brought me full circle, where those children were hurt by the child I had never really been.

I did give up the drugs but by the time I had made the decision to do so it was far too late to reclaim any of the things I had lost or thrown away. Just how far I had fallen became clear only when I woke up in hospital in the middle of February 2006, sustained by a series of plastic tubes attached to various bags and machines. It was 72 hours after I had ingested what remains my final overdose of over-the-counter medication, and this time the pain of withdrawal had been almost too much for my body to take.

42

Fallen

I have fallen.

I have fallen and I am crawling, crawling around in the pitch darkness, darkness I can feel but cannot see, grabbing out with my outstretched arms.

Searching.

Searching. Searching for the happy ending I fear does not exist.

Or does it?

This story of my life is the story of my love. As I scramble around in the dark, I am fortunate that I have found some things that when I landed here I didn't know I was looking for. The further I look, the more answers I find, but still the means to the happy ending eludes me. Answers and understanding do not necessarily solve the problems. In some cases, they pose yet more questions. I have discovered the nature of my demons and I have made an uneasy peace with them, but only time will tell if that peace will be everlasting.

The darkness I now dwell within is a comfort to me and no longer a threat. I co-exist with its uncertainty. I am at peace now with many of the things that at one time or another I permitted to torment my soul. Perhaps, soon, as I search, I will find the courage to take myself on the final journey that I once believed was my destiny. I found my guardian angel but I threw the love she gave me back in her face. Now

I must try to navigate the darkness alone.

I don't feel sorry for myself but I do feel sorrow.

Sorrow for those I have hurt and disappointed. Before I sleep, in the here and now, I pray to the God I know does not exist that tomorrow will never come. Tomorrow brings no respite from the waking torment of today, which itself has offered little chance of escape from the certain torture of tomorrow. If I am to be cursed with another 40 years of this self-destruction, then I must keep searching for a way to allow my instincts to overcome my impulses. So far I am a survivor, but surviving is not the same as living.

I have, on far too many occasions, grabbed heartache from the jaws of happiness. All my life I have craved love, a pure love that I needed to survive, and yet when it found me and I recognised it, I was unable, truly unable, to accept it.

No more.

I am falling once again, falling in so many different ways.

But perhaps that is no bad thing.

I am falling.

Falling for the final time. Falling in a way I should have fallen a decade and a half ago.

Falling truly and hopelessly in love.

Falling in love with the angel who chose to love me so many years ago. I am nothing without love. I only see her image through the darkness yet every time I encounter her I fall that little bit further in love with her.

I have had years to fall this way but something prevented me.

That something was me.

Finally, truly, deeply, I am falling in love.

With a clear head and a swollen heart that informs me that I am profoundly in love with the angel who became my partner, my wife, espoused until I broke the bonds. My angel.

But now I am alone.

This solitude must be for a reason!

I have been falling all my life, ever since I fell from the womb of my mother 39 years ago. There was a time when I must have been at the top but I have no recollection of that time. Now I am so far from the top I can only hope for its continuing existence as I strive to get back. I will. I know I can't fall for ever. No longer do I want to smash my body and soul. I want the descent to end so that I can be left in peace to find my peace. I do not want to die and now, after all that has happened on the way down, at last I am certain I *do* want to live.

I *do*.

But how will I hold this feeling, how will I exorcise the demons and move upwards? I need a tool, I need something to help me, something I can always rely on that isn't drugs or sex or love that I'll always question.

I need something for me.

There is something in my hand.

A weapon.

It has the power to heal me: it's a scalpel, I will cut the demons out; no, a syringe to suck them from my life's blood; no.

It is a pen.

It is the implement of my salvation.

And now I am writing, and in my concentration I look upwards and I see it, small at first but there it is, a star, the first ray of light for a long, long time. I will use this weapon to nurture it, to allow it to illuminate my path. It is at the top and I am on my way to meet it.

I am writing faster and faster as the demons flow from the nib, inky black upon the page and never to return back inside. The ink is as black as the story it tells from my head. Flowing down my arms and out through the pen at the end of my fingers, it all courses from me as I scratch and write.

Once it was in me and now it is leaving.

Going for good. No room for bad. Faster and faster I write. And now, as I near the end of its course, the demons have been slayed. I am victorious. For once I have finished what I started, and even when the going got so very tough, I carried on and out of the (black and) blue. The side effect of this addiction is the death of the past of a man that is no longer me. I stop writing.

But only for a while.

I am no longer dominated and encased by darkness. But I must continue to search. I search as I climb. I do not trip and I do not falter.

I do not fall.

I will not fall.

Ever again.

Epilogue

2008

So, what now?

Throughout my whole life, I had felt alone. There has always been one way of softening many of the blows, though, and that was through the physical act of writing.

When I awoke on that cold February morning in the Royal Infirmary in 2006, I knew I had a choice to make – sort myself out or go under for ever. It was my last chance and I knew as the fug was clearing from my mind that it was one I had to take. With nothing save for a blank page and a fistful of black ballpoints, I embarked on a brutal voyage of honest self-discovery while looking for meaning in my past, a past that I knew would bear heavily upon my future. I had reached the most isolated of signposts on an unfamiliar pathway. Like everyone, I knew not what the future would hold but I had to attempt to influence it in a positive way. Oddly, though I felt physically dreadful and mentally exhausted, I grew optimistic. It was time.

Writing has been something that, up until now, has remained a very private process. When I initially embarked on writing this *thing*, it wasn't a book as such. I was at my lowest point and my reasons for writing were purely personal and I intended for them to remain that way.

I was sorry.

Not for me but for those I had hurt along the way.

I'd never really known what it was like to feel – truly feel – regret and remorse. When those emotions finally hit me, I had no idea how to channel and express them. And if, as they say, a week is a long time at the top, it's a veritable eternity at the bottom. So, it follows, I had what felt like an agonising eternity. The original handwritten manuscript of around 206,000 words was written between 8 May and 19 August 2006, and although I can never pinpoint the moment when the pen took control, it certainly did. During that unfeasibly hot Edinburgh summer, I underwent a personal metamorphosis of massive proportions. In short, stripped bare of any preoccupations, I was able to finally be me.

At the beginning of the writing process, I was still on probation in respect of the events in late 2004/early 2005 and my probation officer asked if I was finding it cathartic. At the time, my answer was a categorical *no*. I was forced to relive some very painful events and felt a great deal of guilt that often resulted in some heaving sobs and feelings of emptiness, but at no time did I nurse a desire to put an end to the process. The explanation and apology was all-important. As was the completion of a worthy project for the first ever time in my life. I had to prove I wasn't a failure.

I had committed many erroneous acts and somehow the mistakes I had made had come back to exact their payment – a payment I was only too aware was long overdue. Now, however, I feel I've paid my dues.

For somebody who had a passion for writing but not necessarily an insight into the machinations of the writing business, I have been fascinated with the literary requirement to be portrayed as sympathetic. This has been the most difficult component of the process so far, given my initial premise of undiluted honesty and a personal requirement to retain my humility and integrity devoid of self-sympathy. I made choices and it is only right and proper that I accept responsibility for those, both good and bad. A big boy did do it but this time he didn't run away! While I do not ask for your sympathy, I implore you not to judge me too severely: you cannot judge me more harshly than I have myself. It might be correctly assumed that I am reluctant to impose the burden of blame onto others for many of my travails. Yes, there were some things that I was never in control of but that is in the main irrelevant. If I were to adopt an attitude of 'Oh, poor me', this whole thing would be nothing more than self-indulgent artifice and I am at great pains to avoid that.

Previously, when reprimanding my kids for some trivial misdemeanour or another, I had always said there are two ways to do things in life – the easy way or the hard way. It finally dawned on me that I had throughout my lifetime constantly been choosing the latter. The more I wrote, the more my life began to unravel and this period was a time in my life which was as pivotal as the death of my grandmother way back in 1976.

In the initial stages of the writing, I was taken back to that most important of times and before too long I realised I had never gone through the mourning process, and so there I was, a 37-year-old man, grieving as a child should have done 30 years previously. Thankfully, I am now at peace with that period, as I am with many of the other things I have documented here.

One of the most important relationships I was able to address was that with my mother. When it became apparent that publication was more than just a whimsical fantasy, there opened up a frank dialogue that has proved beneficial to both of us. I did not wish to demonise my mum. Children can't see things from the perspective of their parents – why should they? – but nor do parents necessarily realise the effect their actions are having on their children. Being a parent isn't easy. I should know. It'd be fair to say that I haven't always been a natural but it's a role into which I'm constantly growing. Through my own experiences, I'm much closer to understanding what my own mother went through during those bleak days of our joint past. Left high and dry, virtually penniless, with a couple of young kids, my mum did what she believed was best. Looking back on things, looking back on life, I'm convinced that there was no malice in her actions. I know all too well how anger and frustration can take hold over someone. The point of my journey of self-discovery wasn't to vilify my mum (or anyone else) but to try to achieve a greater insight into why I had chosen to make the decisions that I did.

As you'll have worked out by now, I was indeed (and freely admit to being) the definitive 'defiant little bastard'. I haven't necessarily changed, although these days I tend to be stubborn or contrary more on behalf of others than myself. When I believe that people close to me are being wronged in some way, my heels still dig in and, to some extent, that's what I've been doing since childhood. My mum was the first figure of authority I encountered and from an early age I knew how to upset her. Even though I knew the consequences could be severe, I strode on regardless. This was my flaw – a flaw that continued to dog me for almost four decades.

I'd be a liar if I said I didn't blame my parents for some things in my life – my mum for her presence and Ray for his absence. It was always easier to believe that my failings were their fault but there comes a threshold in everyone's life when they have to realise that personal responsibility applies to them, too. I also realise that in the early 1970s poverty was hardly exclusive to our house, nor was I the only wee boy without a daddy around.

As I write this, I've arrived at where I want to be with my mum. Over the last 18 years, we've learned to accept each other's idiosyncrasies and as a result our love doesn't hurt as much any more. We speak at least once a day, we enjoy each other's company, we laugh, we politicise, we moralise and we still indulge in the odd joust or two; both of us will retain that feisty streak until the very end and that's how it should be.

Without my mother, I wouldn't be here. I'm not simply being over-dramatic when I say that my mum saved my life and, in effect, saved me from myself. In the aftermath of my absolute descent in the early part of 2006, Mum supported me in every way imaginable. I wouldn't change her for the world. The burden of debt I owe her will be one that I will bear for ever. Even in the knowledge that some of the contents of this book may not put her in the greatest of lights, she has remained enthusiastic and encouraging throughout (even though she tells me she will never read it). At a time when it mattered, she came up trumps and while it may have taken a long time for me to enjoy the deeply held friendship (which matters more to me than any familial label) I have now with my mum, it truly was worth the wait. As a tribute to her, I'll paraphrase one of her many quirky clichés: 'I've changed what I could and forgotten what I can't.'

When I say I love my mum, I mean it. She remains amongst that very exclusive band I am proud to call my friends. And when you hit the bottom you find out very quickly who your friends really are. As a result of this, I do not relinquish my friendship cheaply any more. I like to think I'm worth more than that.

My kids in both camps are loved. I am in regular contact with my two eldest sons but I have seen Amy only once since 30 December 2004 and my youngest son a handful of times in the same period. I am, however, kept updated as to their welfare and I respect their mother's motives for this temporary estrangement. But I would be a cold-hearted bastard and a liar if I said that I do not miss them. It is only fair to mention here that I hold no grudges or harbour resentment towards anyone who in the past contributed to my downfall – life is way too short for bitterness and it is never productive.

Now I live quite contentedly with three cats, all of whom enhance my life way beyond their knowledge; they have even cured me of my fear of rodents (aye, big tough guy, right enough!). Yes, I miss certain people but perhaps it is safer for me to live as I do. No longer do I feel alone, though. My life is enriched by people who want to know me for who I am, not necessarily for what I can give them, and that is something I value highly. Every day, I rise early, eager to absorb and enjoy every new experience life throws my way, even the banal and mundane. When I laugh now, I mean it. I feel it. And I love it. No longer is humour a means of defence. It is a delicious indulgence that continues to taste better and better.

In the summer of 2006, I returned to further education in order to access a gateway to higher education, and having achieved that I now find myself studying in the grandiose surroundings of my home town's esteemed university. I am as astounded by that as I am proud of it. On that morning in the Royal Infirmary a few months earlier, if someone had said to me I would be where I am today, I would have hollered for immediate medical assistance as that someone would obviously have been in need of more (or indeed less) strong medication – such was my outlook at the time.

Now, as a student of literature, one of the recurrent themes is that of the 'fatal flaw' and the question of its existence outside the literary world. I would have to answer that in the affirmative but add that this flaw is also one that can be repaired and improved upon.

There are certain incidents and events that I no longer think about. I only acknowledge their presence in my life. I have neither the desire nor the inclination to elaborate further, as through the writing I have dealt with them and learned in my own way to live alongside them. I am very loath to 'victimise' myself. Playing that role holds little appeal. Yesterday cannot be changed but it is no longer. What matters is today and tomorrow, until, of course, they too become yesterday and are superseded by another today, and so on and so forth.

If you have read this far, then I am sincerely grateful for your investment, be it one of time, emotion or plain hard cash. I can only hope that if my story has in any way been enlightening, educational, inspirational, motivational or entertaining, then I am pleased. If just one person can avoid the pitfalls I have encountered by recognising some of the feelings I have described (and I know this sounds contrived and pretentious but it's the absolute truth), then it's been worth it. Even if you have got this far and hated it, then that is also fair comment. Your opinion is as valid as that of anybody else.

Perhaps I have many more mistakes to make, but as I approach my fifth decade on the planet I would hope that when I have some dilemmas to deal with I will make a judicious evaluation and choose the easy way. I'm far too old for any nonsense now!

And while I may never unkill the thing I love, I am humbled and pleased that I did not die.